BOO
BUILDING

BY LUKE BOSS

Booty Building
By Luke Boss

ISBN: 978-1-3999-0683-8

BOOTY BUILDING

The Gluteus, aka ass, booty or butt, is a distinctive part of the body that is often admired. Each one on this planet is unique as they all come in different shapes and sizes. Getting the 'perfect' butt is a growing trend, especially in the western world.

GETTING THE PERFECT BUTT

Some people want a bigger ass. Some want a smaller ass and less fat stored. And some are happy with the size, yet they just want it to be firmer, toned and a more defined shape without opting for the 'massive' trend.

Celebrities across the world influence this perfect booty trend: JLo, Beyoncé, the Kardashians and Hugh Jackman to name just a few.

Many people see this trend as a bizarre obsession and don't realise that there is more to gain from looking after our buns than you think. There is more to it than just to look better and stand out from the competition! There are also astronomical benefits to our physical and mental health!

Many people are resorting to paying for expensive cosmetic procedures on their butts, such as butt implants or removal of fat from their ABZ to their butts (each to their own). Whereas building your butt through working out HARD and eating right is sustainable and comes with great pride!

CONTENTS

WHO I AM & WHY I DECIDED TO WRITE THIS BOOK

My name is Luke Boss, this is my first book, and I am a Glute-Crazed Booty-Fanatic! I am a personal trainer and I run my own fitness classes as well as coach people 1-2-1 to help them get the body they desire. Seeing my clients transform their bodies is one of the highlights of my work.

By far, my favourite part of my own body to train is my gluteus muscles. I like to train them 2 - 3 times a week depending on the amount of spare time I have.

Up to the age of 18 I had been overweight pretty much all my life. I once weighed 16 stone and I was very unfit. It was in LA when I decided I finally needed to do something because I could never be topless, no matter how hot it was, as I felt so ashamed. There were so many hot guys and girls roaming about scantily clad on the beach or wearing revealing clothing on West Hollywood main street. No way was I going to show my body next to theirs.

One summer (after LA) was spent constantly walking up and down hills, as well as doing ab exercises in my bedroom, sometimes up to 500 crunches a day. I would also starve myself, and the few times I did eat it would be low calorie junk food. I did, however, bring my weight down to 13 stone by the end of the summer, which was a huge personal achievement for me. But I was constantly told I looked anorexic and that I had a 'flat butt'. I eventually decided to hit the gym, but with no clue how to train in order to get the body I wanted.

Despite having many things going on in my life, I always exercised at least 5 days a week. In 2014, whilst training in the gym, I had a reality check: 'Why aren't I doing this as a career?'

Before I enrolled on my personal training course, I looked online to see how I could transform my body into what I wanted it to be. I learned how to gain muscle on the whole of my body and I would read the training plans of bodybuilders and try them out for myself.

Within 6 months I had transformed my body substantially. However, one body part has always been close to my heart, and that is my glutes – not physically, obvs!

One day a week I train my glutes with heavy weights at my local gym, doing either squats or deadlifts followed by isolation exercises and finishing off with some high intensity plyometrics (explosive power training) exercises. If I have extra time in the week, I'll add another heavy session. I'll also do an upper body session one day a week at the gym. One day a week at home I do some bodyweight glute exercises as a top up to what I did in the gym.

I'm not saying that my body and booty is perfect, but I have come a long way compared to what I was. Don't get me wrong, I'm not saying you have to do all this to get the perfect butt. I would recommend 3 or more days a week of training at the gym will be perfectly ample for you to see a difference.

The bum is the cutest and most beautiful part of the body in both males and females, and not just sexually. Having said that, someone may have a cute face, a lovely personality, and if this cuteness continued to their butt, they would be my perfect match!

When I am in the gym, I often get annoyed when I see the same ladies just doing cardio and guys just training their upper body and ignoring their potentially lovely booties.

It has been on my bucket list for a while to write my own book. My aim is for you to be confident enough to develop your own training and diet plan that will make a difference. You will also learn what it takes to get your desired ass-cheeks.

As a qualified personal trainer, I have seen how people over the world have been following the trends set by celebrities and written books about how to build the perfect butt. However, they are almost all aimed at women's glutes, and therefore men miss out. This prompted me to write my own Booty-Building Book for both men and women.

There are approximately 7.594 billion people in the world, and that means there are 7.594 billion pairs of buttocks! I think it's safe to say this book has its purpose!

As I am not a keen reader myself, my book is designed to be as clear and direct as possible. What I set out is easy to follow and you can do so at your own pace.

I am aware and perfectly happy that the majority of people reading this will be females due to the current trend set by many A-listers such as JLo and the Kardashians. There is also more pressure on women due to them storing more fat on the butt than men, as well as many of them wearing more revealing swimwear and underwear than men. However, men also have so much to gain as, like women, they have an ass! I believe it is as masculine for men as it feminine for women to have well looked-after butts. We sometimes see naked men's rears in movies and these guys have been picked to show their beautiful booties for a reason.

No matter whether you are male or female, gay or straight, having a nice booty will be another attractive feature of your body for yourself or other people to look at, whether you are fully clothed or completely naked.

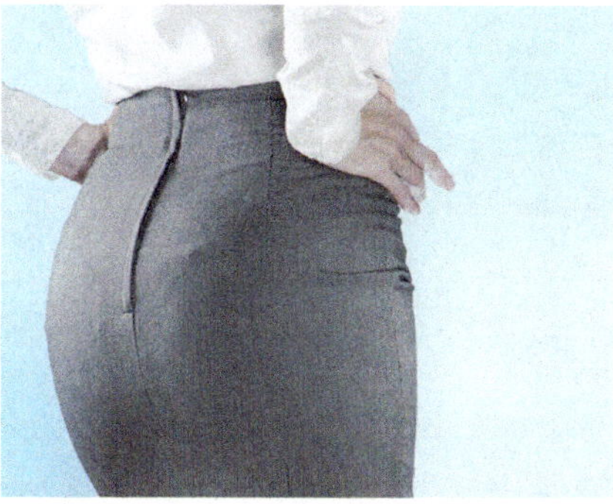

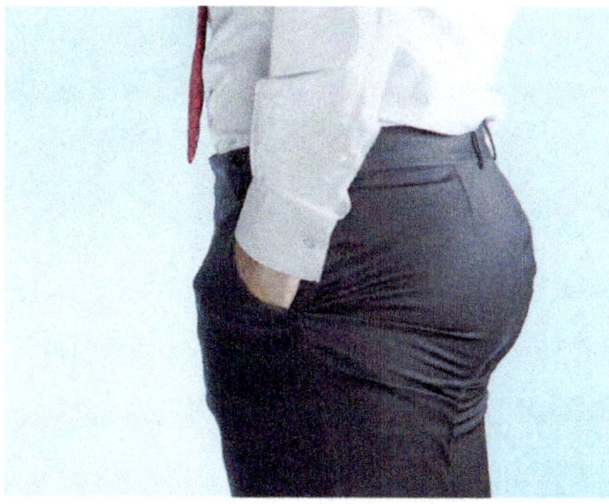

STRUCTURE OF THE BOOTY BUILDING BOOK

Firstly, I will talk a bit about the booty. (My favourite body part – I love mine now!) I will also go into some history about the booty culture.

Then I will give information on the anatomy of the glutes and lower body – this is a lot more important than you'd think! I will cover aspects such as skin, hormones and how characteristics such as gender and race make all glutes different and unique.

Nutrition and diet will be next. This is very important as we want to build, maintain and shape our asses, but we want the correct gains, shapes and sizes. We don't want a high Tum:Bum ratio – we want the opposite! There will also be some nutritious and tasty recipes for you to try.

Then it is all about the training and exercises, telling you which muscles each exercise works. I will show you how to keep a training workout journal, which will help motivate you to set yourself ambitious goals. Also, you will learn how to structure your workouts.

Finally, it's the 38-session programme! This is where it's less reading and more ACTION!

Time to get working on those butts!

CULTURE AND HISTORY OF MALE AND FEMALE GLUTES

The idea of the perfect size and shape of booty has varied throughout history and varies across cultures. Also, there are distinct differences between the anatomy of male and female glutes.

CULTURE & HISTORY

Throughout the world, what is considered the perfect booty differs and the culture of celebrity also plays a major part in what is considered ideal.

WOMEN

Women have a reputation for taking great pride in working their glutes. However, the big booty culture has not always been popular. Having said that, women's glutes have been deemed elegant and beautiful all the way back to the Ancient Greek times.

In recent years, however, the aspiration to get a juicy and firm ass has become a more desirable asset than the flat stomach trend. Butt is considered the new breast and the big ass/tiny waist is now extremely popular and considered a very attractive body frame. Not just to the lady or girl who wants it, but by what men like to see on a beautiful looking lady.

A major factor in the big booty trend is the celebrities, whether they are popstars, movie stars or reality tv stars. Not only do stars like JLo, the Kardashians, Beyoncé, Nicki Minaj, and Shakira have the desired booty and figure people want, they promote it actively and take pride in their shape. This pride has a massive influence and inspires young girls and women.

Music videos are a major contributor to the current trend. Amazingly, music videos centred around the beauty of female booty have been around since the 1960s. However, the 1992 hit 'Baby Got Back' by Sir Mix-a-Lot proved to be a major dedication to the beauty of curvy women and bigger butts. The video starts with two young women degrading a beautiful girl with a big booty, defining her body as "gross" and saying she "looks like a prostitute". It highlights how, back then, it was not only far less popular to have a rounded ass, but unfairly frowned upon, along with the many other prejudices and body fascism there were back in the day. There were many other popular rap and R&B hits back in the 90s that promoted big juicy asses, such as 'Back That Azz Up' and 'Thong Song'. Nowadays there is a booty-inspired music video revolution, particularly by female artists promoting the beauty of not only their own butts, but big butts and curvier bodies in general. These include 'Anaconda' by Nicki Minaj and 'Booty' by JLo.

Instagram is the major social media platform for the trend due to being based on images. #Squats has reached a massive 16.3 million mentions on Instagram! And #Booty also has a big juicy mention of 4.6 million.

Men are commonly asked "Boobs or Butts/Bums?" According to many findings, it is very close to 50/50. This doesn't mean that men love one and not the other. It is like asking me whether I fancy George Clooney or Ryan Reynolds. I fancy them both! Having said that, a study from the University of Buenos Aires found that 59% of men prefer women's butts over their boobs.

Of course, women don't just take pride in the appearance of their hard-earned booty to attract or impress their partners, they also do it for themselves!

South America has a big, big, BIG reputation for its massive booty culture, existing long before the UK and US. Brazil is known for its annual butt-centric 'The MissBumBum competition', where hundreds of women all over Brazil head to San Paulo to compete.

This trend is not going away!

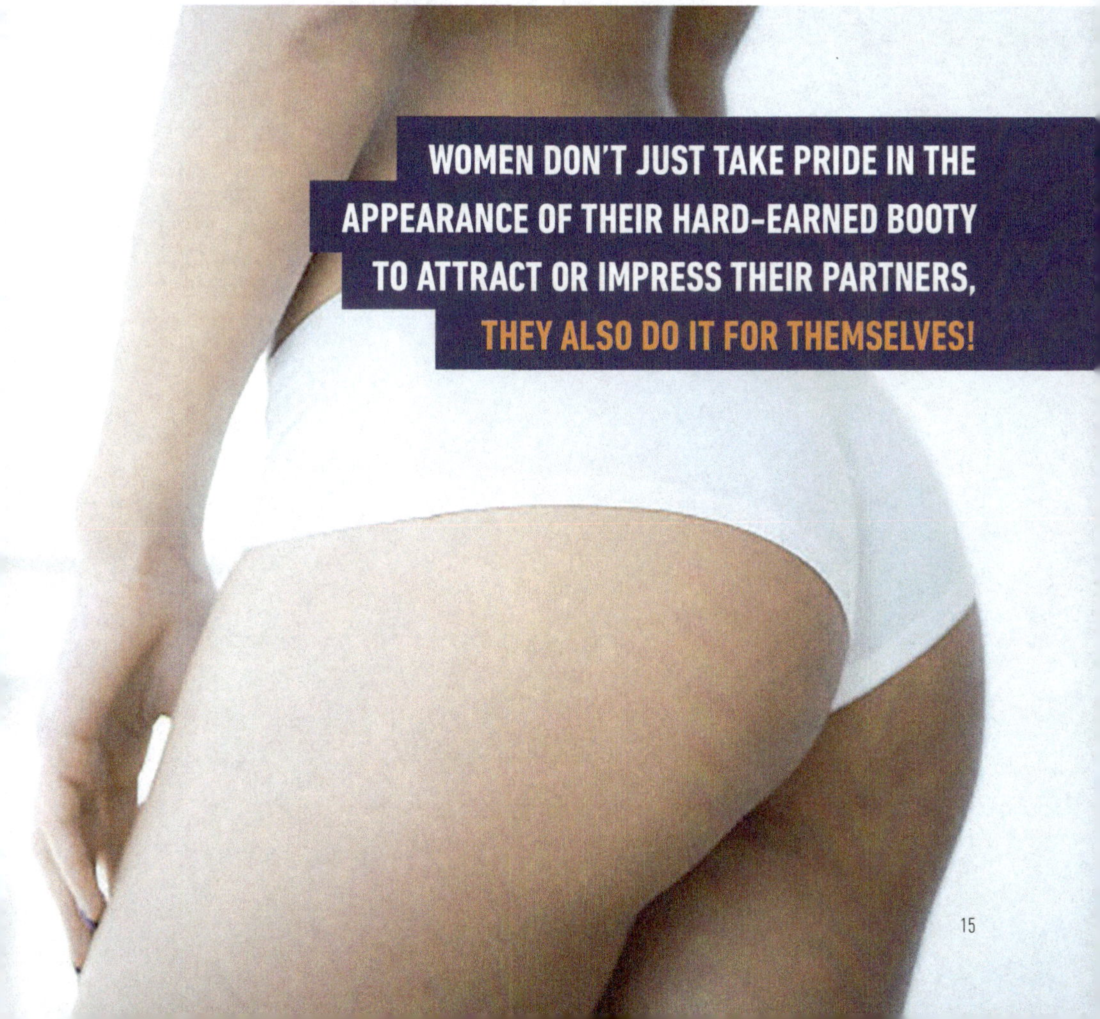

WOMEN DON'T JUST TAKE PRIDE IN THE APPEARANCE OF THEIR HARD-EARNED BOOTY TO ATTRACT OR IMPRESS THEIR PARTNERS, THEY ALSO DO IT FOR THEMSELVES!

MEN

There isn't the booty renaissance culture for men like there is for women – unless I have anything to do with it! The male booty, however, has its place in history and current culture and is slowly gaining momentum. There's the trendy and sexy term 'bubble butt' to describe a defined and firm butt of the male species.

In history, the male ass has got its famous figures, such as the iconic Michelangelo's famous statue of David. Ancient Greece displayed a beautiful selection of men's glutes – I think it's safe to call it a glute-crazed era!

In films, men have had their fair share of iconic butt scenes – remember the *Terminator* movie? Yes, the character was a robot, but it was played by a very hunky Arnold Schwarzenegger! Also, remember Hugh Jackman's sexy rear nude scenes in *Wolverine*? I strongly believe we need even more man-booties in the spotlight. Not just because I am gay, or because I'm a glute-centric booty fanatic. But because I feel that the male booty should be valued in this way. In popular comedy culture, male butts have a reputation for 'smelling' or 'farting' and nothing else. In reality, guys have the same digestive system as the girls! Their butts are just as beautiful!

Although there is nowhere near as much research into why women are attracted to male butts as there is for why men are attracted to female booties, there is a theory that it is less about the butt itself, and more about how a toned butt affects how the man walks – so you love to watch him leave! Having said that, there are surveys (and I can confirm from asking my gal pals) that say a nice butt is an attractive feature in a man.

Regardless of your gender or sexual orientation, give your boyfriend/girlfriend, husband/wife, f**ckbuddy, or even that cute stranger in the grocery aisle something to look at when your back is turned!

WHY YOU SHOULD WORK YOUR BUTT

.01

.02

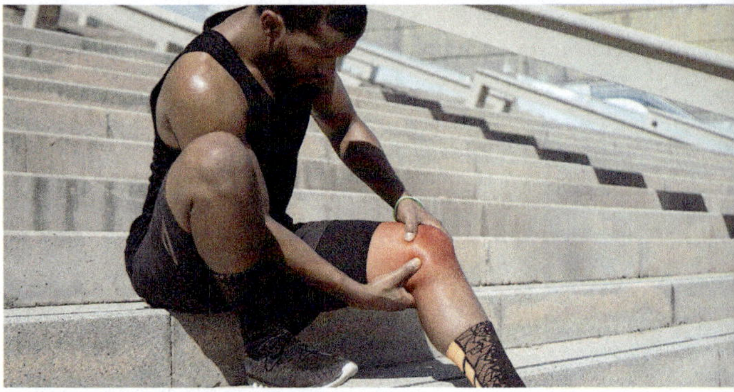

.03

FACT 01: THE GLUTEUS IS THE LARGEST MUSCLE GROUP IN THE HUMAN BODY AND ONE OF THE STRONGEST

The gluteus is a dominant muscle group of the body and has huge potential to grow bigger and bigger. However, if not worked, it also has potential to store masses of fat deposits (more so in females) due to sedentary lifestyles and/or poor diet. Another thing that can happen in both males and females is an undesirable 'flat butt'. This often happens with inadequate diets, too much of the wrong exercises and not enough rest.

FACT 02: A WEAK BUTT CAN LEAD TO INJURY

In particular, this can happen when you don't spend enough time strengthening it. One reason why they are such an important muscle group is because a healthy butt has the ability to carry a lot of weight compared to other muscles. When the glutes aren't strengthened enough you put more pressure on other muscle groups – hamstrings in particular, but also the quadriceps, calves, lower back and some joints. Therefore, a strong butt helps other muscles.

FACT 03: YOU'RE CONSTANTLY USING YOUR GLUTES

Gluteus muscles are considered one of the 'grafter' groups of muscles as they are used in many daily activities. Your gluteus helps support your body when you stand, helps when you push yourself off the ground, and improves your balance. This therefore greatly impacts many daily and weekly activities, such as walking your dog, getting up the stairs, and most sports, such as swimming and golf.

ANATOMY OF THE GLUTEUS

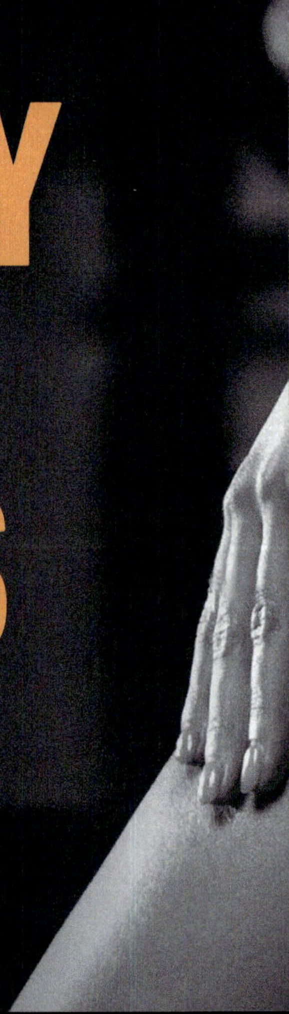

f you are wanting to change the appearance of your butt, it is mportant to understand the anatomy, especially considering the size of the gluteus. However, it can be fascinating learning what makes each ass so different to others! The gluteal muscles are a group of three muscles: the Gluteus Maximus, Gluteus Medius and the Gluteus Minimus.

GLUTEUS MAXIMUS

This is the largest and most superficial gluteus muscle. Also known as the bulk of the power! Training this muscle will have a HUGE impact when it comes to improving appearance.

Stronger muscles like the gluteus maximus generally need to be larger. By keeping it strong and well worked out, this will also give you a more round-shaped ass. This muscle is worked the most in well-known exercises such as squats, deadlifts, hip thrusts and glute bridge. Also, it's heavily worked in moves that involve moving the hips backwards, such as plank leg lifts and scorpion kicks. (Don't worry if any of these names seem completely foreign to you. I will go through each of these exercises later in the book.) This muscle also plays a role in the adduction and abduction of the leg and hip rotation.

TIP: Training the gluteus maximus significantly cuts the risk of glutes sagging. We don't want that!

GLUTEUS MEDIUS

These are the upper muscles and are a major factor in the appearance and build of the butt. They are a deeper muscle than the maximus and are also an extremely important muscle involved in the abduction and rotation of the hip. This and the gluteus minimus assist each other for the medial rotation of the thighs and hip.

When we perform many glute exercises, we use a lot of thigh and hip medial rotation.

FACT: Abduction occurs when you move your leg out sideways from the body, such as side leg raises and firearms. Adduction is the opposite movement to abduction, where the movement means to draw the legs inwards or closer to the centre of the body.

GLUTEUS MINIMUS

It's the smallest – but that doesn't mean it's not important! This is the deepest of the three muscles. It's located even deeper, behind the medius. It works together with the medius to perform the abduction of the leg. It is also one of the muscles responsible for medial rotation of the thigh.

FACT: Medial rotation (also known as internal rotation) is rotation that occurs towards the centre of the body.

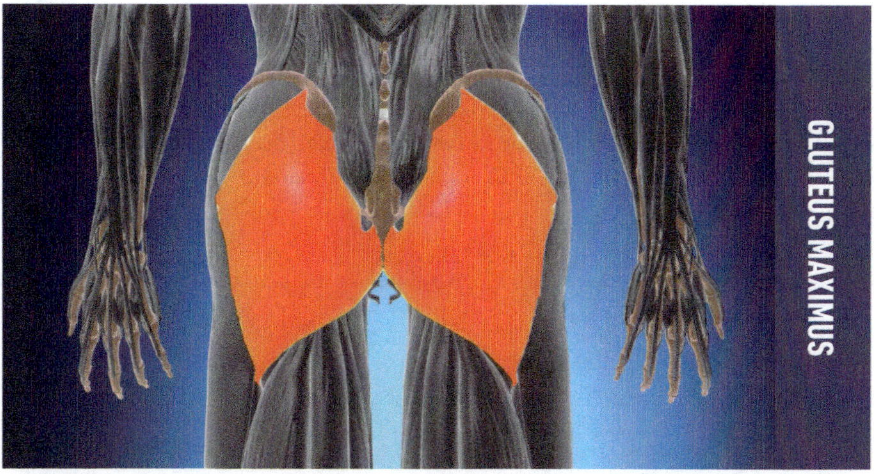
GLUTEUS MAXIMUS

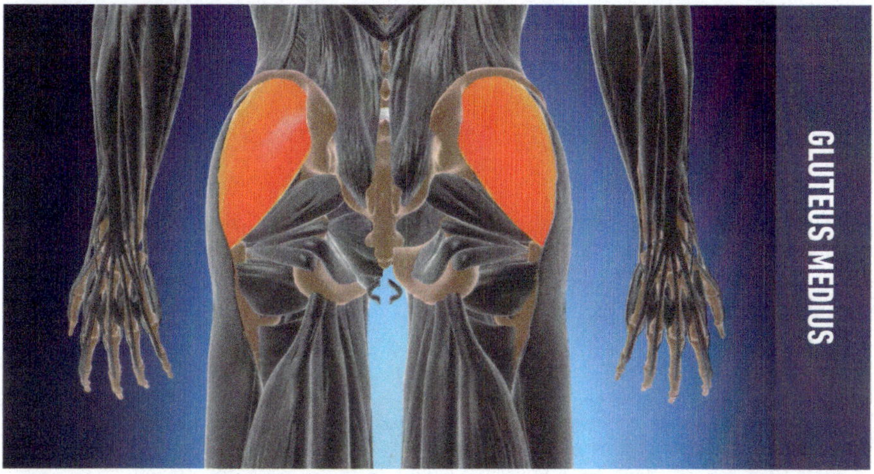
GLUTEUS MEDIUS

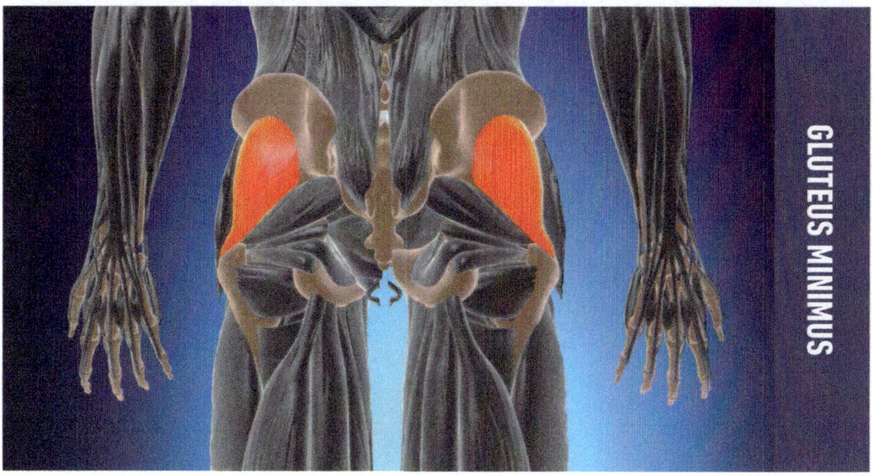
GLUTEUS MINIMUS

FACTORS WHICH SHAPE YOUR BUTTOCKS

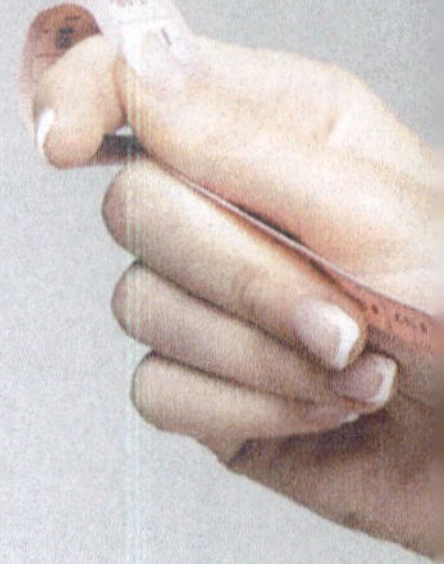

The shape, size and appearance of your butt varies because of a number of factors, including gender, race, diet and lifestyle. In addition, the shape of a male and female butt differs because of factors such as the structure of the pelvis and differing hormone levels.

However, you can change the shape by following a certain diet or by performing certain exercises. The type of exercise and diet depends on the shape you want.

For example, a peachy butt is a butt that is perfectly rounded like a peach. Whether you are male or female, having a peachy ass adds definition, wanted curves (yes, guys as well!) and character to your gorgeous body. To get a peach ass you need to work your ENTIRE ass, therefore the gluteus medius needs to be incorporated into your workouts just like the gluteus maximus. You will also need to consume reasonable nutrition and follow healthy lifestyle habits.

YOU CAN CHANGE THE SHAPE OF YOUR BUTT WITH DIET AND EXERCISE

PELVIS

FACT: The shape of your pelvis is something you cannot change!

The pelvis is largely what makes the male ass different to the female ass. The pelvis is the bone that forms the shape of your hips and base for your booty.

The average female pelvis is considerably wider than the male pelvis. This is to allow for childbirth and it causes the femur (or thigh bones) to be positioned further apart. The width of the female pelvis is the main reason why the female butt is typically wider than the male butt. As a result, it is considered feminine to have a wider shaped butt.

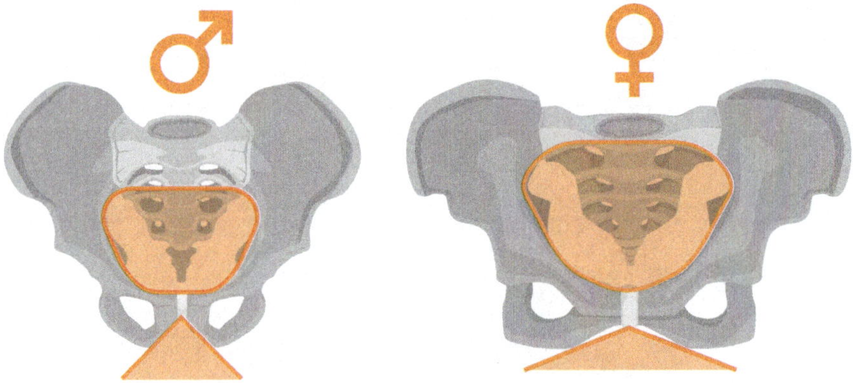

The male pelvis is generally taller and narrower. This leads to a squarer butt shape and often referred to as a 'hunk' butt, as seen in movies such as *Terminator*.

Many people believe that it is healthy and ideal to get rid of all fat from their butts, but this isn't true! Subcutaneous fat is found around most of the body. However, there is a larger amount stored in the glutes.

This fat is also known as adipose tissue and sits as a layer above the gluteus muscles. Having a healthy layer of this fat helps create a nice shape. Fat is completely natural, and by exercising and having a good diet we normally maintain a healthy level of gluteal fat.

Having a healthy layer of subcutaneous fat on the butt makes many life chores easier, such as sitting down (especially on hard seats!), bending over to pick something up, or running after your dog. Also, it can look very healthy and sexy indeed!

FAT DISTRIBUTION AND RACE

The depth of fat layers differs due to men and women having different hormones. But more about hormones later.

If we lose fat, we lose it all over the body, and vice-versa if we gain fat. However, with a healthy diet and the right exercises, you can lose extra fat in the parts you don't want, such as the abdominal areas, whilst keeping a healthy layer of fat in the booty.

Your race/global region also has an effect on how much fat you store in the gluteal region, particularly for women. Different fat distributions occur according to the climate. In hot countries mainly in Africa and the Caribbean, the fat gained by women is centred around the buttocks. Mediterranean women are known to gain excess fat on their hips, and women in certain South Asian countries are prone to gaining considerable fat around the navel.

This variation in distribution avoids covering woman with hot coats of fat that would be difficult to bear and inefficient for thermoregulation during hot periods, whereas in cold countries the fat distribution is more uniform. This is to provide better protection during the harsh winters.

FACT: The ass fat layer is much larger in females than males.

CELLULITE

Cellulite is considered the bane of many women's lives as it affects women to a far greater extent than their male counterparts. It is a common condition mainly found in the glutes and hips in which the skin has a bumpy appearance.

This happens when fat deposits manage to push through the connective tissue beneath the skin. Women are most likely to experience cellulite as they age, and it peaks near menopause.

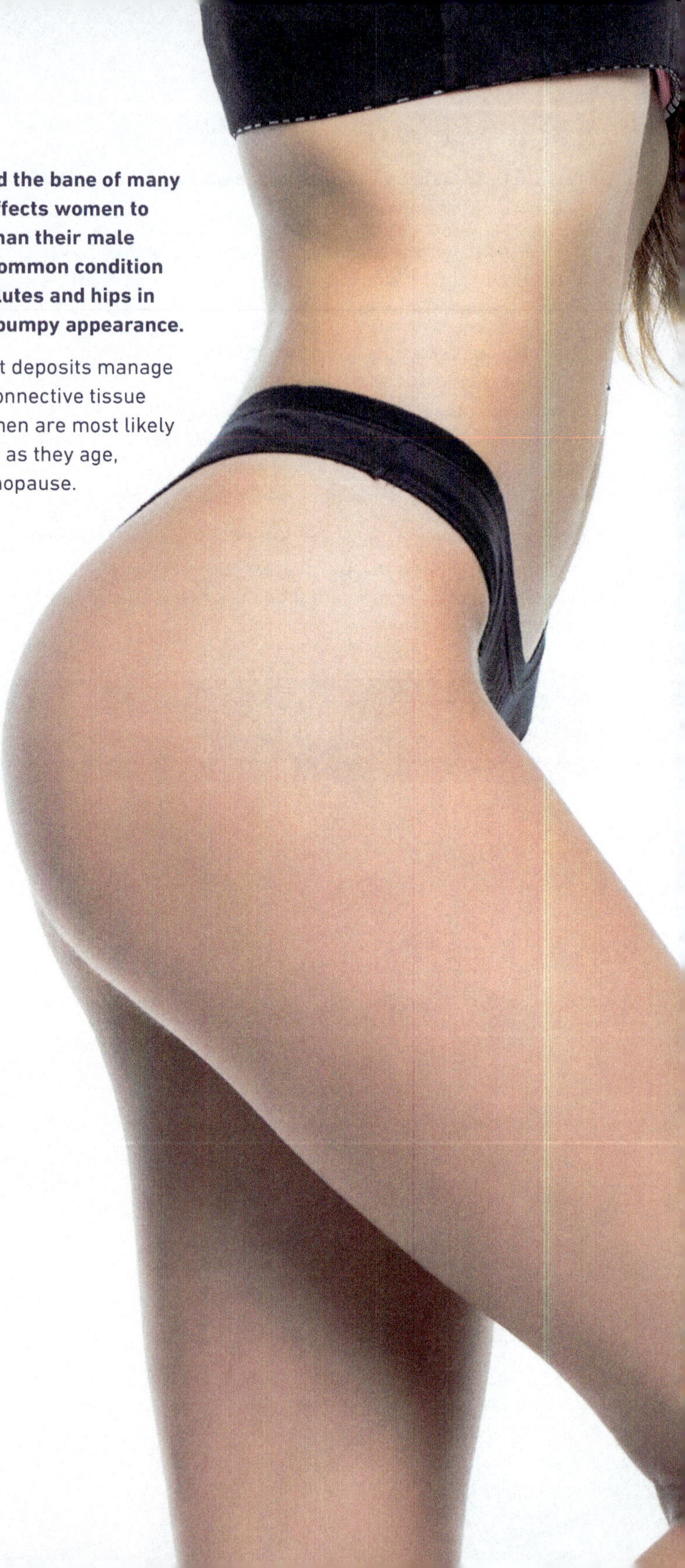

Hormonal changes, especially a decline in oestrogen (or testosterone in men), often contribute to changes in circulation and a reduction in collagen production. Fat cells increasing in size and quantity, combined with a thinner collagen layer, increases the risk of cellulite.

Another major cause is the slowdown of fat metabolism as we age. However, having a sedentary lifestyle along with a poor diet are major factors in the production of cellulite, especially as our metabolism slows and our hormones change, as it will increase fat deposits.

Therefore, making healthy lifestyle choices, such as exercising and eating healthily (especially foods with good fats, vitamins and fresh food) will greatly reduce the risk of cellulite forming.

Cellulite is not considered dangerous, but many people see it as unsightly. I'm here to tell you that people (women especially) are more at risk of getting cellulite as they age and we can't do anything about that. However, we can easily slow down the risk by exercising and eating healthily.

SKIN

The skin on the buttocks is viewed as the icing on the cake in terms of the appearance of the butt. A well-toned and shaped male or female bum would not be the same without beautiful skin. When we are born, we all have perfectly soft and smooth skin on our buttocks. As we age, we start to lose the elasticity and thickness of our skin, and when we get to our 40s, we are prone to the dreaded sagginess of the once lovely smooth glutes.

Whilst we cannot do anything about getting older, we can drastically reduce the ageing of our skin (especially the skin on our glutes) by leading a healthy lifestyle. This is where DIET and EXERCISE comes in yet again.

Having a healthy diet is VERY important. This is because older skin cells are shed and replaced by newer ones. However, to maintain a speedy regrowth, vital nutrients are needed. These are antioxidants, omega-3 and omega-6, and multivitamins. For skin to stay moist and flexible you need to stay hydrated by drinking at least six glasses of water a day.

Exercise helps our lovely skin, and especially aerobic exercise has been proven to promote blood flow, which increases the rate of new cell growth and the production of natural oils found in the body. By maintaining an exercise regime, skin will be more flexible and supple, and this will prevent wrinkle formation.

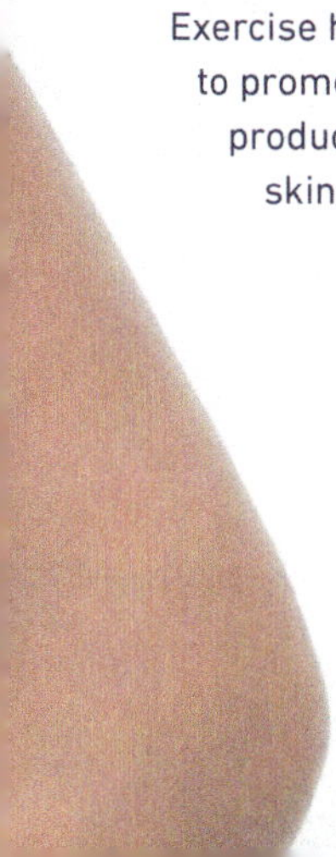

HORMONES

Earlier, I explained that hormones are another factor that determines why male and female buttocks are shaped and structured differently. Men and women produce different levels of certain hormones. I am not going to go through all the hormones produced in the body, but I will mention the hormones involved in the development of butt growth in males and females.

FEMALE HORMONES

Certain hormones not only play a part of the shape of the butt but also the breast area and overall feminine curves which so many women desire to achieve.

Oestrogen – The main sex hormone in women, mainly produced in the ovaries and possibly the hormone most associated with women's bums and curves. Not only is it most responsible for the development of breasts, bigger and wider hips and an increased amount of body fat on the butt, but also the fat distribution on thighs and hips. Oestrogen is not considered a muscle growth hormone, but it is an extremely healthy hormone with many benefits to the body, such as healthy fat loss. In fact, women with healthy levels of oestrogen are less likely to put weight on the abdominal area. By exercising regularly and having a healthy diet, oestrogen will greatly help your feminine figure and your butt.

Progesterone – Works with oestrogen to maintain female reproductive health and develop female characteristics. Progesterone, however, is more responsible for curves in the breast area rather than in the hips and booty. There are benefits to this hormone, as it is useful for keeping fat off the waist as well as keeping excess fat off the glutes. Therefore, this gives curves all over!

Testosterone – The main male sex hormone. It is mostly associated with men, yet females produce testosterone, but much less. It enables the body to build some muscle and tone after a workout. However, having too much testosterone in women is not ideal for the desired feminine booty. For women, having an excess of testosterone in the body blocks butt, hip and breast growth. Testosterone belongs to a group of hormones called androgens. If you struggle to grow your butt after working out hard, a possible reason could be down to excess androgens in your body. There are anti-androgen supplements available that could block excess androgens, but make sure you seek advice from your doctor so you know it is safe and for peace of mind. Please note there are risks in taking supplements to alter your hormones just as there are gains.

Prolactin – Commonly associated with periods and the breasts. It is more important for breast growth rather than butt growth as it enables excess oestrogen to go to the breasts rather than the butt. There are anti-prolactin supplements available to make extra oestrogen go to the butt instead. However, again seek medical advice as there are risks.

MALE HORMONES

Testosterone – The main male sex hormone and a steroid hormone, mainly coming from the testicles. It develops secondary male characteristics such as male fat distribution and is also a major contributor to muscle growth. By having high testosterone and growth hormone levels, strength and muscle mass increase, which can only mean more muscle on the bum!

Other benefits are body fat reduction, greater concentration, increased energy and a higher sex drive. Testosterone may not be the hormone to shift excess fat from the core to the butt, but it is the hormone to put a large amount of muscle on the biggest muscle group of all! Healthy levels of testosterone are also linked to more defined abs.

I only recommend building testosterone naturally, which can be done in many ways. This can be from regular exercise (especially strength and bodybuilding), getting at least 7 (preferably 8) hours of sleep each night, minimising stress levels and adequate nutrition (plenty of good quality protein, carbs and fat).

Guys, if you really feel you need to take supplements to build adequate testosterone levels, then please be aware that there are health risks just as there are gains. The benefits include increased muscle mass, better fat distribution, bone mass and improved sex drive.

The negative effects include a shrinking of the testicles, increased mood swings, increased acne, increased risk of blood clots (deep vein thrombosis and pulmonary embolism) and more so do your research!

Oestrogen – In men, oestrogen is not the ideal hormone to have in high levels, as when oestrogen increases testosterone decreases. It is healthy to have some oestrogen, but at a low oestrogen-testosterone rate. Too much oestrogen can result in man boobs, loss of muscle mass, depression, low libido and difficulty in getting or maintaining an erection.

Men can boost their testosterone-oestrogen ratio naturally by regularly lifting weights (especially squats and deadlifts), eating healthy protein, carbs and fats (eggs are proven to be a very good way to boost testosterone), limit stress and cortisol levels, taking vitamin D and getting at least 7 hours of sleep. As men hit 30, testosterone starts to slowly decrease, so it is especially important to live a healthy lifestyle. Excess alcohol (especially beer) and drug abuse can increase oestrogen levels so try to stick to drinking in moderation and avoiding recreational drugs.

MALE AND FEMALE HORMONES

Growth hormone (HGH) – Produced in the pituitary gland in both men and women. It is a very important hormone for butt growth as it is responsible for stimulating the growth of new cells, tissues, organs, cartilage, bone and ... muscles! It is also the anti-aging hormone. As we age, growth hormones decrease, but by making regular healthy lifestyle choices we can prevent them from decreasing at a fast rate. Healthy sleep levels, exercising regularly (especially resistance training), limiting stress and cortisol levels, eating healthily and not smoking are good habits to improve growth hormone levels. Another way is to make sure you get enough amino acids. This can be done by increasing protein intake or by taking amino acids tablets found in many health stores. Other positive effects of this hormone are increased protein synthesis, increased lipolysis (decreases fat) and it also supports the pancreas and its production of hormones such as insulin and glucagon.

Protein synthesis is the process of building new proteins. Muscle protein synthesis is the process of building muscle protein. As you improve muscle protein synthesis, you build muscle.

FACT: There is a process called muscle protein breakdown. THIS ISN'T YOUR FRIEND!

Muscle protein breakdown is the opposite process which decreases protein synthesis. The goal is to have muscle protein synthesis processing at a faster speed than muscle protein breakdown so that you build mass.

Cortisol – The body needs this hormone, despite the bad reputation it has for encouraging weight gain and reducing muscle growth. Produced in the adrenal cortex in response to stress, it helps us deal with direct stress by shutting down certain functions in the body such as the immune system. Cortisol levels are normally high in the morning, which is ideal for the body at the start of the day when we are generally more productive. This helps us when we go to work or to the gym.

The ugly side to cortisol is when the body produces too much of it, especially at prolonged stressful periods.

Cortisol partially shuts down the immune system during stressful periods, which then makes the body more prone to becoming sick. More importantly, when it comes to muscle growth, excessive cortisol inhibits the uptake of amino acids into the muscle cells as well as reducing protein synthesis and muscle tissue growth. This all relates to the growth and transformation of our muscles, especially our bums! Too much cortisol affects the entire hormonal system, such as insulin, growth hormone, testosterone and oestrogen, which are all important for the build of our BOOTIES. Blood pressure also goes up in the presence of elevated cortisol.

Excessive cortisol eventually leads to effects on mental health, such as mood swings, anxiety and depression. In a nutshell, cortisol at the right level is definitely our friend, but with too much of it, it becomes the enemy!

There are many ways you can control cortisol. Have a healthy diet (extra veg, fruit, fibre and antioxidants), exercise regularly, reduce stress when possible, limit caffeine and get enough sleep. Sound familiar? You'll learn more later in the book on how to deal with stress and getting a proper diet.

LIFESTYLE

There are many things we do in our lives that reduce the chances of getting the body we want, which includes lovely bums! Many of these have already been mentioned, but I thought it would be good to go through each in turn.

SMOKING

If you are serious about getting the perfect booty, then next time you reach for a cigarette, you might want to think again. We know there are lots of risks associated with smoking so I'm not going to bore you. However, as previously discussed, you'd be surprised what smoking can do in terms of cellulite and the gluteal skin.

Cigarette smoke reduces blood vessel flow and weakens and disrupts the formation of collagen. This allows for the connective tissue to become more stretched and damaged and for underlying fat to show.

And if you want your glutes to stay smooth and soft, then here's a reason why smoking won't help. Cigarette smoke contains carbon monoxide, which displaces the oxygen in your skin and the nicotine reduces blood flow. This then dehydrates skin and leaves it dry, giving it a less appealing colour. Wrinkles also occur quicker.

SLEEP

A lack of sleep can seriously affect your gluteal goals.

FACT: Lack of sleep is the enemy of fat burn and muscle growth!

After we work out, the body is mainly transformed when we sleep. The growth hormone is released mostly overnight and this hormone naturally helps us burn fat, tone, build muscle and age slower. Lack of sleep will also lower testosterone levels in men and oestrogen in women, which as you know are sex hormones that give us natural characteristics and prevent illnesses. They also play a very important part in building our booty and the rest of the body! Lack of sleep has also been known to lead to affect insulin levels, which can lead to diabetes.

FACT: Lack of sleep has a major effect on our workouts!

So, whether you want to build or trim your booty, sleep is important. With a sleep deficit, you will also be mentally and physically fatigued before you even reach the gym. A lack of sleep will raise the cortisol hormone (stress hormone) beyond healthy levels. Remember, cortisol is a steroid hormone and too much can reverse the positive effects of the growth hormone; it also enables the body to gain weight on the face and abdomen.

STRESS

As so many of us lead such hectic lifestyles, it is common for us to get stressed. But excess stress creates a barrier to our gains. Excess stress means excess cortisol. It has an impact on sleep patterns, and eventually our willpower with regards to eating a healthy diet and going to the gym. There will always be some stress in our lives. However, there are many ways to drastically reduce the chances of getting too stressed.

HOW TO REDUCE STRESS

1. Change your eating habits and eat more whole foods, fibre and essential nutrients. Limit cortisol and inflammation by avoiding trans fats (commonly found in fried food and convenience food like microwavable popcorn), food high in unnatural sugar, and limit caffeine and alcohol intake.

2. Meditation helps put daily anxieties to one side so that you can see and do things with a new perspective. Many people meditate to improve their mental health and use it as a technique to deal with daily stress. However, it can also be used to improve many bad habits, such as an erratic sleep pattern, unhealthy diet, infrequent exercise, smoking or drinking too much alcohol. You can attend sessions run by professionals, go to social meditation groups or download many meditation apps to your phone or tablet, so there is no excuse not to give it a go.

DIET AND NUTRITION

It's all about eating the right foods at the right times. We all have cheat days and its perfectly ok to have them, but most us have them more often than we should. The key is to eat fresh and lean as the norm and don't let cheat days become a regular thing.

FACT - What you eat is crucial to your goals

Many people think that eating fast food will make their ass bigger in a good way – this is not the answer! If you were to get your protein from hamburgers, your carbs from fries and your sugar from chocolate, the majority of fat gained would go to your waistline. Any weight gained on your ass will mainly be flab. Not to mention bingo wings! And for men, you will get moobs!

Get yourself into the habit of eating the right portions of clean and lean protein, slow-releasing carbs (like sweet potato and brown rice) and a mix of monounsaturated, polyunsaturated and saturated fats (more about them in a bit). Fruit, veg and fibre are also important. Here is a list of ideal food that will aid the appearance of your ass.

PROTEIN

Protein is well known as being very important for muscle growth – which means our butts! In a nutshell, protein provides the building blocks for muscle growth and helps the body repair and grow new muscle tissue. It is tricky to consume enough protein to allow for sufficient muscle growth, even if we put protein in all our meals. One thing that could be damaging for booty growth is eating a calorie and protein restricted diet, which would lead to the breakdown of muscle tissue, especially the glutes! This would truly be demoralising after endless booty grafts in the gym!

I always recommend your protein being as LEAN as possible. Lean protein can be plant- or animal-based. Although high in protein, it should be low in saturated fat and added carbs. An example would be a chicken breast, tuna or steak with little fat. Oily fish is often considered a lean protein despite being higher in fat than other sources of fish, and this is because the fats are mainly unsaturated and high in omega-3, which is anti-inflammatory.

Examples of plant-based options would be tofu, beans and tempeh. Some beans have higher amounts of carbohydrates than others, yet these carbs are completely natural and carbs are also important.

I'd say the ideal amount of protein for an individual is 1 gram of protein for every pound (lb) of your body weight. For example, if you weighed 160lb then it would be advised to have 160g of protein.

However, you can increase it to 1.5g per lb if you are super determined for mass results or if you want to lose a lot of weight whilst getting lean. But please do not overdose on protein as it has been known to lead to unwanted fat gain.

So which foods should you eat to increase your protein intake?

Eggs – A very good source of energy; try to consume them in the morning as they help to power you throughout the day and during your workouts.

Fish – Some fish are high in lean protein and also high in omega-3 fatty acids, which are excellent for gaining the right weight (gain lean muscle and losing bad fat). Tuna, salmon, squid, and mussels are all high in protein and if you want more omega-3, then eat mackerel.

Chicken – Low in cholesterol and a lean source of protein.

Steak – Try to opt for steak with less fat, or trim the fat if at home. This red meat is also a very powerful source of protein and a perfect post-workout reward. You can always replace steak with lean beef.

Tofu – A very good source of protein for vegans as it contains all the essential amino acids. It also contains iron, zinc and many fantastic minerals and vitamins such as vitamin B1. Another recommended vegan alternative is tempeh.

Beans – Another efficient vegan-friendly option. They are low in fat, high in fibre, and rich in protein and amino acids. Try to go for dried beans and boil them yourself. Many canned beans, such as baked beans, have lots of added sugar in the tomato sauce. There are lots of beans to choose from, such as black eyed beans, chickpeas, kidney beans and haricot beans. However, one very impressive bean is black turtle beans. I was amazed by the nutritional value when I first heard about them, mainly because they are very high in fibre and very high in protein. Therefore, they would be a fantastic snack to nibble at all day, as it is often difficult to get enough fibre in a diet, particularly if you lead a busy life.

Protein shakes – Fast-acting sources of protein that absorb into your muscles quickly, especially after workouts. They help with building muscle mass, maintaining blood sugar levels and decreasing production of cortisol. There are many different sources of protein powder, such as whey, casein (a dairy protein), milk, beef, and vegan options, such as soya, pea and hemp. Whey is probably the most commonly used protein powder. However, if you want a protein powder to have before bed then opt for a slower acting protein powder such as casein.

Cottage cheese – If you feel hungry, this is an ideal snack. It contains casein, which is a slow digesting dairy protein, therefore it's not a bad snack to have in the evenings. It also contains a lot of good bacteria.

Yoghurt – Greek and Icelandic yoghurts are a great way to get a good amount of protein in the morning and by adding fruit or oats you also get your carbs. You can add fibre with chia seeds or pumpkin seeds. Some brands of Greek yoghurt have added sugar and flavourings which will make the protein source less 'lean'. But if you wanted to sweeten up your Greek yoghurt, I recommend you go for plain yoghurt and sweeten it your own way with natural sugar, cinnamon or organic honey.

CARBOHYDRATES (CARBS)

It is a lot easier to get enough carbs than it is protein. Carbs are often considered a big no-no when dieting. However, the truth is that there are good carbs (complex carbs) and bad carbs. Good carbs assist in muscle growth and hormonal growth, whereas bad carbs store as the wrong sort of fat. If you want your butt to grow to its full potential, then good carbs are considered even more important than protein, especially after a workout.

Carbs are often known for playing the role in providing the right hormonal environment for growth. Try to cut out bad carbs or limit them to treat days. Bad carbs are junk food, white bread, white pasta, sugary cereals, sweets/candy, packet noodles and macaroni cheese, crisps/chips and fries.

These are typically packed with sugar and/or salt and have little nutritional value. These carbs also increase your insulin level, which can make your blood sugars spike, and this promotes the storage of fat cells, particularly in the belly area. White potatoes are a tricky one as they are a vegetable and contain essential nutrients, yet they make us very full and tired quickly. Here's a list of the good carbs we're talking about:

Oatmeal aka porridge – Contains micronutrients that help increase muscle mass for the butt as well as being good for keeping you full until lunch. Also good for cholesterol levels and the heart. A butt carb!

Sweet potato – Very healthy as it is packed with vitamins C & B6, and potassium. It has been known to add healthy weight to our desired areas of the body – the butt.

Wholewheat – Cut out white bread and swap it for wholewheat bread. It has far more fibre, keeps you fuller for longer and is good for adding healthy weight to the butt.

Quinoa – A good alternative to white rice. It's naturally gluten-free and contains some essential amino acids as well as vitamins. It also contains a good amount of protein, which is handy for vegans and vegetarians.

Brown pasta and rice – Easier to digest and contain far more of the healthy carbs needed for butt muscle mass as opposed to their white rivals. They both are also very good sources of fibre.

Carbs are also considered very important for muscle recovery, so you will need more carbs on training days than rest days. If you buy a protein shake after the gym, then opt for a 'recovery shake' and save the total protein shake for later. Alternatively, add some oatmeal flakes to the shake to increase the carb ratio and create your own 'recovery shake'! Carbs should take up a minimum of 40% of your total calorie intake if you are dieting at a calorie surplus or maintenance (whether you're eating more or near the same number of calories as you are burning – I will explain more later). If you are dieting to a surplus, I'd advise 50% of the total diet to be of carbs.

FRUIT AND VEGETABLES

Fruit and vegetables can help you stay healthy and should be part of your diet. They also contribute to a beautiful butt! You should aim to get at least 5 portions of fruit and vegetables a day, with each portion being about 80g (potatoes, yams and cassava don't count as they are high in carbs).

Try to eat as much of a variety of fruit and veg as each of them contains different vitamins, fibre and minerals, including folate, vitamin C and potassium. They are also a fantastic source of dietary fibre. On top of all this, they are usually low in fat and calories – just don't fry them or roast them in litres of oil! They can be fresh, frozen, dried, juiced or canned.

Green vegetables – So important for butt growth yet light in calories – Win-Win! This is because they are packed with antioxidants, vitamins, minerals and fibre. They keep you full for longer, which makes you far less likely to crave junk, and help improve your mood as they are a great source of folate. Most greens even contain a reasonable amount of protein compared to the few calories they contain. They are also good for cholesterol, bone health and skin. Stock up your fridge with these as you need them! The greens I most recommend are broccoli, brussels sprouts, kale and spinach. They are called superfoods for a reason!

Fruits – They may be a sugar, but they are a natural sugar and it is healthy to have some sugar in our lives. They are a good source of nutrients such as potassium, vitamins, folic acids and antioxidants. This means they are helpful for blood pressure, cholesterol and healthy skin. And more importantly, they are an excellent source of energy! But avoid fruit juices that are made from concentrate.

Root vegetables – Such as squash, carrots, beets, parsnips, turnips and pumpkins. Like green vegetables and fruit, they are also packed with many minerals and vitamins such as potassium, calcium and iron. They generally have more calories and sugar per gram than green vegetables but are fantastic for keeping us feeling full and sending healthy weight to the bum!

FATS

As said already, fats are really important for butt growth, whether you want to increase, decrease or maintain your butt size. Fats are far more calorie dense than protein and carbohydrates but if you have the right sort of fats (polyunsaturated and monounsaturated fats), they give a variety of essential nutrients and are perfect for gaining healthy weight in the booty whilst losing the fats we don't need.

FACT: Polyunsaturated and Monounsaturated fats are types of unsaturated fats which are considered good fats for our diets.

Polyunsaturated fat includes omega-3 and omega-6 fatty acids and these acids are essential for brain health, nerve function, muscle strength and blood health. This fat helps lower the bad cholesterol (LDL) in your blood.

Monounsaturated fat is also a fat that helps protect your heart by maintaining the levels of good cholesterol (HDL) whilst reducing the levels of bad cholesterol.

Too many people have little or no good fats at all, which may be a cause of certain health problems in the world, particularly high cholesterol. Dietary fats are essential to give our bodies energy as well as to support cell growth. They also help protect our organs and keep the body warm. Fats also assist with the production of essential hormones for butt growth. I advise you to consume between 0.3 - 0.5 grams of fat per pound of bodyweight.

There are ongoing debates on the health benefits and the downsides of saturated fats such as cream cheese, whole milk, and butter. Having reasonable amounts, such as a light spread of butter on a sandwich or having some cheddar on your salad, should be no problem. But don't have them every day – or worse, with every meal – as there is an increased risk of high cholesterol. Avoid cooking with saturated fats when you could be cooking with dietary fats such as olive oil. Saturated fats don't contain the nutrients for the right and healthy sort of weight gain. Opting for monounsaturated and polyunsaturated fats, such as olive oil, raises the good cholesterol (HDL) and lowers bad cholesterol (LDL). One type of fat to watch out for is trans fats. They raise bad cholesterol, contribute to arteries being clogged up and therefore increase the risk of heart attacks and strokes. They are also a major factor in high obesity rates in the world. Try to limit pies, cake, cookies, biscuits, margarine, doughnuts, microwaved meals, fried food and frozen pizzas. These foods are normally packed with trans fats. I'm not saying don't treat yourselves now and again, but don't let it be on a daily basis.

Here are some of the good fats we need to build our booties!

Oily fish – Packed with omega-3 fatty acids, which are known as good fats. Good fats help reduce bad fats from arteries. Oily fish are high in calories but they are packed with nutrition and so helpful for cholesterol and blood pressure. If you want to get a larger butt, you have to eat more calories than you use, and eating oily fish will not just help that, they will also give you useful nutrients that transfer the weight to the butt. These are far more efficient calorie sources compared to the 'empty calories' you get from junk food. Examples of oily fish are mackerel, sardines, salmon, trout and herring.

Nuts – Packed with good fats and are also a good source of protein. They help good cholesterol and are rich in vitamins and minerals. Avoid nuts that are covered in salt. Fantastic choices for nuts, but by no means a full list, are pistachios, cashews, almonds, walnuts and Brazil nuts.

Avocados – Love them or hate them, they are a fantastic choice if you want to build a healthy mass on your bum. They contain a lot of vitamins, minerals, fibre and amino acids and have the added benefit of being fantastic for your skin! They are also brilliant to cook with!

Seeds – Like beans, seeds are an excellent sources of omega-3 and omega-6 fatty acids, fibre and protein. Perfect for recovery after a workout! You can add them to porridge/oatmeal, smoothies and cereals for extra nutrition. As with beans, there's loads to choose from, including pumpkin, hemp, flaxseed and chia seeds.

Coconut oil – Contains medium-chain triglycerides which help build lean muscle, encourage fat loss and improve health. There are debates as to how healthy it is, with it being very high in saturated fat. Adding a teaspoon to your protein shake will help your goals, but as it is very high in calories, be careful how much you use.

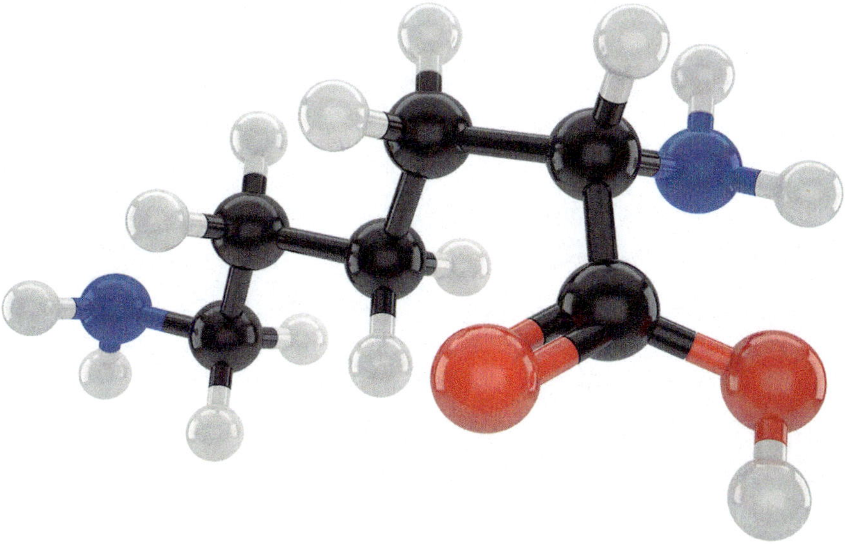

AMINO ACIDS

Amino acids are organic compounds that combine to form the building blocks of proteins. The human body uses amino acids to make proteins which help the body break down food. They enhance workout performance, promote recovery and help build muscle.

There are 3 groups of amino acids – Essential, Non-essential and Conditional.

The majority of the amino acids we require come from our diet. Depending on our lifestyles and the food available, it can sometimes be a challenge to consume the right quantity and variety required. I am not going to bore you by going into each one and describing its effects but I will describe the acids that I personally recommend for training and exercise.

Branch Chain Amino Acids (BCAA) – These three acids are essential, meaning they can't be produced by your body and must be obtained from food. BCAA supplements have been shown to build muscle, decrease muscle fatigue and alleviate muscle soreness. These three acids are called leucine, isoleucine and valine.

L-Lysine – A supplement I choose to take as it helps the body promote collagen, helps reduce anxiety, supports the immune system (reduces cold sores) and helps the body absorb many minerals (calcium, iron and zinc).

L-Glutamine – This is a good one for gym-goers due to the role it plays in aiding muscle repair. As you work your muscles, you destroy them in the process, and this amino acid helps your body and muscles recover and therefore grow. This acid also helps reduce cramps, aches and pains after working out. Glutamine also encourages growth hormone levels, which is particularly important for increasing muscle volume and size.

CREATINE

This isn't an amino acid but is a very popular sports supplement used to increase muscle mass and improve strength and exercise performance. It is a substance that is found naturally in muscle cells. It helps your muscles produce energy during heavy lifting or high-intensity exercise. This then alters your body so you are more likely to do more intense physical activity and therefore gain more muscle mass and/or fat loss.

Supplementing with creatine can result in significant gains in muscle mass – and therefore booty mass! This can range from people completely new to working out, all the way to elite athletes. There are also many health benefits from taking creatine. These include lower blood sugar levels and improved memory and brain function.

When taking creatine, there is a loading and maintenance phase.

Loading phase – When you first take creatine, you take a higher amount for a small period of time (ideally for 5-7 days) before you reach the maintenance phase. It is recommended that between 15-20 grams of creatine is advised for the first 5-7 days. Ideally evenly spread out throughout the day into 4-5 doses. Taking it before and after a workout is recommended as this can help deliver creatine to the cells more effectively after a heavy gym sesh!

Maintenance phase – After the loading phase, you should continue to take creatine at a reduced dosage of 5 grams (give or take) but for a longer period than the loading phase (typically for another 1-3 months). Again, try to take the doses before and after a workout.

It is then recommended that after loading and maintenance, you come off creatine for at least a month, though many people leave it a lot longer. People usually see the extra gains from taking creatine 6-8 weeks after the first dosage.

Try to consume a glass of water with each dosage of creatine.

TIP: Please seek professional health advice before taking any supplements.

HOW MANY GRAMS ARE IN WHAT?

These are estimations for popular sources of protein, carbs and fat. Some foods, such as bread, will not be as accurate due to the variations available e.g. wholewheat bread.

PROTEIN

100g Chicken Breast	31g
100g Chicken Thigh	25g
One Large Egg	7g
4oz Ground Beef	29g
4oz Steak	28g
4oz Lean Lamb	28g
100g Tuna	30g
100g Shrimp	24g
100g Scallops	21g
100g Mussels	24g
100g Salmon	20g
100g Squid	18g
100g Fillet Fish (Cod, Haddock, Catfish)	15g
100g Pork Loin	27g
100g Ham	21g
1 Cup of Whole Milk	8g
100g Cottage Cheese	11g

VEGAN PROTEIN

100g Tofu	8g
100g Chickpeas	19g
200g Kidney Beans	24g
100g Black Beans	21g
100g Lentils	10g
100g Cashew Nuts	18g
100g Pumpkin Seeds	19g
100g Walnuts	15g
1 Cup of Soya Milk	8g
100g Almonds	21g
100g Pistachios	20g

FAT

1 Tbsp Olive Oil (Or Extra Virgin Olive Oil)	15g
1 Avocado	15g
1Tbsp Coconut Oil	14g
100g Mackerel	25g
100g Salmon	13g
100g Almonds	49g
100g Cashew Nuts	44g
100g Walnuts	65g

NOTE: Coconut oil is a saturated fat but works well as an unsaturated fat like extra virgin olive oil.

CARBOHYDRATE

100g Apple	14g
100g Banana	23g
100g Blueberries	14g
100g Cherries	12g
1 Fig	8g
100g Grapefruit	11g
100g Grapes	16g
100g Mango	16g
1 Medium Orange	15g
100g Pear	15g
100g Potato	17g
100g Sweet Potato	17g
100g White Rice	28g
100g Brown Rice	23g
100g Egg Noodles	25g
100g White Pasta	5g
100g Brown Pasta	26g
100g Broccoli	7g
100g Cabbage	6g
100g Sweetcorn	19g
100g Parsnips	18g
100g Carrots	10g
100g Beetroot	10g
100g Oatmeal/Porridge	12g
100g Quinoa	26g
100g Wholewheat Bread	13g

CALORIES

This is when you need to decide what you want to achieve with your booty. We are all aware of calorie counting and the need to be aware of how many calories we should be consuming. But how do you work that out?

BASAL METABOLIC RATE

Basal Metabolic Rate (BMR) is the number of calories your body burns all day at rest. Once you understand your BMR and know your own number, you can use it as a benchmark to achieve a healthy weight and/or get the great booty you want.

BMI CALCULATOR

You can work out your BMR with this equation:

Men

BMR = 66.47 + (13.75 x weight in kg) +(5.003 x height in cm) - (6.755 × age in years)

Women

BMR = 665.1+ (9.563 × weight in kg) + (1.85 × height in cm) - (4.676 × age in years)

However, unless you lie in bed all day, you will need more calories than your BMR. First take into account your lifestyle.

NON-TRAINING DAYS

If your daily activity outside of the gym and work is sedentary (inactive), then multiply your BMR by 1.2. (BMR ×1.2)

If your daily activity outside of the gym involves a lot of movement which keeps you active, or if you stand up all day at work or at home, or if you walk your dog for 30-60 mins then multiply your BMR by 1.375 (BMR×1.375)

However, if your job involves lots of heavy manual labour for approximately 8 hours a day, then multiply your BMR by 1.55.

WORKOUT DAYS

If you also workout you will need to increase your calorie intake even more as you are burning more at the gym.

This depends on how intensely you train. If you train at home using bodyweight or with lighter free weights, you are less likely to burn as many calories and your Maximum Heart Rate is likely to be less compared with if you trained at the gym with heavier weights and more equipment.

MAXIMUM HEART RATE

Your Maximum Heart Rate (MHR) is the maximum number of times your heart beats per minute during exercise.

Calculate your MHR by subtracting your age from 220.

If, for example, you are 35 years old, subtract 35 from 220 to get a maximum heart rate of 185.

If you train at 50-70% MHR for up to 1 hour, then add an extra 15-17.5% on top of your non-training day allowance

If you train at 70-85% MHR for up to 1 hour, then add an extra 20-22.5% on top of your non-training day allowance.

YOUR CALORIES IN RELATION TO YOUR GOAL

The total equation doesn't stop there. You need to adjust your calorie intake depending on whether you want your booty and body to get bigger, smaller or to maintain its size but be more firm and rounded.

TIP: Depending on how you want your butt to look, you will be aiming for a calorie surplus, deficit or maintenance.

Calorie surplus – If you are in lean shape but you want to increase the size of your booty, then you need to consume more than you burn. Work out how many calories you need each day and add an extra 20% of calories on top.

Some nutritionists even advise a calorie surplus of 1000 calories! Of course, this would typically be for a 6ft 3in male who can deadlift 200 pounds! The extra calories need to come from healthy protein, slow release carbs and fats. Make sure you are getting at least 1g of protein per lb of bodyweight at the bare minimum. On non-training days, slightly reduce the amount of carbs you consume. However, protein is still very important.

Calorie maintenance – If you are happy with your weight but you want to shed weight in the areas you don't want excess (like your waist) whilst getting a better-shaped butt, then you need to eat at maintenance calorie levels. This means eating as much as you are expending. Work out how many calories you need and stick with it, ensuring you get a minimum amount of 1g of protein per lb of bodyweight. If you work other parts of your body, then this method can be considered as transformation!

Calorie deficit – Do you want to shed a considerable amount of body fat in areas such as the waist and thighs whilst keeping and toning your glute muscles? This option is for you and is about consuming fewer calories than you use. A warning – do not have the deficit too high; it needs to be a sustainable deficit rate of around 15-20% maximum. On training days, you need to increase your calorie intake due to you burning more calories. One easy way is to eat at maintenance level.

FACT: A calorie deficit which is too high and too fast has been known to lead to fatigue, lower metabolism, muscle wastage and muscle loss!

Once you find out how many calories you need, then try to balance it out evenly between at least 4 meals, excluding pre- and post-workout snacks. Also, don't worry too much about getting it exactly right! It is difficult to keep on track of what you are eating accurately. The last thing you want is to become obsessive and stressed - **life is too short.**

HYDRATION

Try to consume 6-8 medium glasses of water a day on training and non-training days. If you replace all drinks with water so much goodness will happen to your body, especially if your diet is high in antioxidants. Drinking water helps decelerate the aging process by keeping your skin adequately hydrated. It moisturises your skin, which keeps it young, soft and wrinkle-free. Water will also assist the liver and kidneys in eliminating things we don't want in the body, such as toxic substances, waste and excess salt. This will help the body trim unwanted fat.

There are a number of ways to stay hydrated, such as drinking water, or mixing it up a little and adding lemon. However, not all drinks are beneficial and you should limit your caffeine and alcohol levels.

LEMON WATER

If you hate the taste of water and want to add flavour, then add a slice of lemon. Even better, every morning prepare yourself for the day by putting 1 large lemon slice in a cup, fill half the cup with boiling water then fill the rest of it with room temperature water. Avoid flavoured water, including lemon flavoured water.

Lemon contains potassium, calcium and magnesium, all of which are electrolytes, which help with hydration. Lemons also contain pectin fibre, which helps to reduce appetite and suppress cravings.

Lemons contain a lot of vitamin C, which strengthens the immune system and the nervous system and also prevents a rapid increase in cortisol. By drinking lemon water you are increasing alkaline in the body and therefore improving your alkaline:acid ratio. Too much acid in the body is easily done (from excess sugar intake, too much alcohol, lack of fruit and vegetables in the diet), and this increases the risks of certain diseases such as cancer.

CAFFEINE

In moderation (which is about 2 cups a day for the average person), caffeine is a workout's friend. When taken at the correct time of the day, caffeine will increase focus and give energy. Excess caffeine has been proven to increase cortisol levels, raise anxiety and disrupt sleeping patterns.

Having excess caffeine can make you easily distracted in the gym and will disrupt your focus and performance, as well as making you more dehydrated. Try not having your first cup immediately when you wake up; instead, opt for water. Give yourself an hour after you get up so your body has time to wake up by itself and then have your first coffee or tea. If you think the reason you are often stressed is from too much caffeine, maybe just have one cup per day and for the rest of the day have decaffeinated or fruit juice. But make sure you still drink enough water.

TIP: Energy drinks, in my opinion, are not worth it. The very high caffeine and sugar content will make your energy levels boom and bust!

ALCOHOL

When you are on the beach in your bikini (or your Speedos if you're a guy), it looks great to have a cocktail in one hand with your booty on display. And it's nice to put on a pair of jeans (or a dress) that shows your fabulous booty shape, and to go out and let your hair down whilst the odd girl or guy is having a cheeky peek – whether it's turning them on or if they are just admiring your glorious butt!

Life is short. We are entitled to get wasted now and again at parties, on holiday, at weddings, or even when you have friends coming round. However, try not to make a few drinks a night become a regular thing. Alcohol is, at the end of the day, a drug and it has many effects on our bodies – which means our booty.

WHAT ALCOHOL DOES TO THE BODY

1. Raises cortisol and insulin levels whilst slowing down the formation of growth and sex hormones.
2. It's empty calories. They can't be used for anything useful like protein, slow release carbs and healthy fats. This makes it even harder for someone on a calorie deficit plan. Beer is probably the worst alcoholic beverage for empty calories. If you want a drink with less calories, then opt for either gin or vodka with soda or a low calorie mixer.
3. Slows down protein synthesis.
4. Binge drinking will drastically reduce your chances of hitting it big on training days. Your energy levels will be affected and your body will be dehydrated.
5. Increases the risk of cancer and liver disease.
6. Regular heavy drinking can result in alcoholism.

If you can, try to avoid boozing on training days and the day before. Or if you want to, have just 1 or 2 drinks.

BOSS RECIPES

Here are some recipes which are packed with super-nutritious ingredients. I find these recipes comforting and filling. Some are higher protein, some higher carb and some higher fat. I try to use as much as possible of the best types of protein, carbs and fat etc.

SPICY KING PRAWN BAKE WITH COURGETTE

SERVES 6

This is clean food but really tasty.
I enjoy this dish with brown pasta on the side.

INGREDIENTS

- **3 tablespoons of olive or hemp oil**
- **1 large courgette, chopped and diced**
- **4 garlic cloves, peeled and chopped**
- **1/2 teaspoon of chilli powder**
- **1/2 a fresh red chilli, very finely chopped**
- **2 x 400g tins of chopped tomatoes**
- **1 teaspoon of dried basil**
- **1/2 teaspoon of salt**
- **1/2 teaspoon of ground pepper**
- **200g spinach, washed**
- **400g raw king prawns**
- **500g chickpeas, rinsed and drained**
- **250g mozzarella cheese, drained and chopped into strips**

HOW TO MAKE:

Preheat the oven to 190°C degrees/gas mark 5. Heat the oil in a large frying pan over a medium heat. Add the courgette and fry for 6 minutes, stirring occasionally. Then add the chilli, garlic and chilli powder and fry for a further 2 minutes.

Add the tomatoes, basil, salt and pepper and cook for 8 minutes, stirring the ingredients. Then add the chickpeas, spinach and prawns and cook for 2 more minutes.

Tip the contents of the frying pan into a baking dish. Scatter the mozzarella evenly over the top and press some of it down into the sauce. Bake for 20-25 minutes and remove from oven.

Optional: Sprinkle some grated parmesan and some fresh basil leaves to garnish.

Serve and enjoy!

LEAN TURKEY KOFTAS

SERVES 2

This is a far leaner alternative to meatballs. Very low carb if you are on the keto diet.

INGREDIENTS

- **3 tablespoons of olive oil**
- **150g of turkey mince**
- **2 dried apricots, chopped very finely**
- **1/2 red onion, very finely sliced**
- **1/2 teaspoon of dried oregano. You could also use fresh oregano but make sure it's very finely chopped.** (Yes, I keep saying finely!)
- **40g quinoa flakes**
- **1/2 teaspoon of sea salt**
- **1/2 teaspoon of black pepper**

TIP: The onion and apricots must be very finely chopped so that the flavours are evenly distributed throughout the meatballs.

HOW TO MAKE:

Line a baking tray with baking paper. Place the turkey mince, chopped apricots, onion, oregano and quinoa in a bowl with the salt and pepper. Mix thoroughly with a spoon.

With wet hands, divide the mixture by loading a tablespoon and then roll the mixture into meatballs. Place each ball onto the lined tray and refrigerate for an hour. This allows for the meatballs to bind together so that they don't fall apart when cooking.

Heat the olive oil in a frying pan for 5-10 minutes and add the meatballs. Cook until they are golden brown all over and cooked throughout, gently turning over with a spatula (they should take approximately 30 minutes to cook). They are now ready to be served.

Optional: A refreshing green salad of spinach, rocket and lettuce, topped with thinly sliced spring onions lightly drizzled with balsamic vinegar and extra virgin olive oil is a perfect accompaniment.

Serve and enjoy!

SPICY BEEF WITH SWEET POTATO

SERVES 4

This is an Asian-style recipe. I use sweet potato as I find it adds far more flavour, plus it's far healthier. This is also a recipe suitable for the colder months.

INGREDIENTS

- **500g beef sirloin**
- **2 tablespoons of dark soy sauce**
- **2 tablespoons of fish sauce**
- **2 tablespoons of olive oil**
- **3 chopped coriander leaves**
- **1 teaspoon of dried chilli flakes**
- **2 tablespoons of peppercorns, crushed**
- **2 garlic cloves, chopped**
- **350g sweet potatoes, peeled and diced into chunks, not too big.**
- **150ml water**
- **100g spring onions**
- **250g baby spinach leaves**

HOW TO MAKE:

Cut the beef into thin slices and place in a shallow dish. Place the soy sauce, fish sauce, 1 tablespoon of the oil, coriander leaves, 1 teaspoon of black peppercorns, garlic and chilli flakes into a food processor and blend into a thick paste. It's important to make sure the paste isn't watery. Pour the paste evenly over the beef and then toss the beef until both sides are covered. Cover the dish with cling film and place in the refrigerator for 4 hours to marinate.

Heat the remaining oil in a large wok on a medium heat for 5 minutes or until it is hot. Remove the beef from the marinade and cook in the wok for 3 to 4 minutes until browned on both sides. Add the sweet potatoes, the rest of the marinade and the water and gradually bring to the boil. Slightly reduce the cooking heat and simmer for 8 minutes.

Try a piece of potato to see if it's nice and tender. Then add the spinach and spring onions and another teaspoon of cracked black peppercorns. Cook on the same heat until the green vegetables have wilted.

Optional: Serve with shirataki or edamame noodles. Alternatively, serve with brown rice.

Serve and enjoy!

SWEET POTATO GNOCCHI WITH SUN DRIED TOMATOES

SERVES 4

I have not only replaced the white potato with sweet potato to add flavour and nutrition but I've also replaced regular white flour with buckwheat flour, which is higher in protein and fibre. This recipe isn't the quickest recipe to do, but when it's time for dinner it's worth it! The sun-dried tomatoes and spinach, as well as cabbage served on the side provides extra vegetables. In fact, I advise you to serve this as a side dish with the king prawn and courgette bake.

INGREDIENTS

- **3 medium-sized sweet potatoes**
- **120g spinach**
- **2 egg yolks**
- **1/2 teaspoon of salt**
- **1/2 teaspoon of crushed black peppercorns**
- **250g buckwheat flour**
- **2 tablespoons of olive oil**
- **300g cabbage, washed and then chopped, not too fine**
- **2 garlic cloves, chopped and crushed**
- **3 sun-dried tomatoes, sliced**
- **100g parmesan cheese for grating**

HOW TO MAKE:

Preheat the oven to 200°C, line a roasting tray and place the sweet potatoes in the oven for 50 minutes or until they are tender. When cooked, remove and leave them to cool. Wash the spinach under a tap in a sieve and squeeze out excess water. Chop the spinach finely and set aside.

Once the sweet potatoes are cooled down, cut them in half and scoop out the flesh into a large bowl. Mash until smooth, add half the sun-dried tomatoes, chopped spinach, egg yolks, and salt and mix well. Gradually add the flour in small batches until you have a workable dough. You don't necessarily need to add all the flour.

Flour the surface of your worktop and divide your dough into 4 portions. Roll each portion into a long strip approximately 1.5cm thick. Cut each strip into individual pieces around 2cm long. Shape each piece into a nugget and place them all in the fridge for about 30 minutes to firm up.

Bring a large pan of salted water to the boil. Add the cabbage and boil for 3-5 minutes. It is important that the cabbage does not go soggy. Remove the cabbage and place it in a sieve to remove excess water, then leave to cool slightly. Keep the water you cooked the cabbage in on a medium to high heat and bring to the boil.

Remove the gnocchi from the fridge. Add to the water and cook until they rise to the top. Don't allow them to stick together. This should take 5 minutes or less. Using a spoon, remove each piece from the pan and place on a cooling rack to dry.

In a large frying pan, put the oil on a low to medium heat and cook the garlic. Add the other half of the sun-dried tomatoes and cook for 2 more minutes. Add the gnocchi to the pan and fry until it is lightly coloured. Then add the cabbage for a further 3-4 minutes or until it is slightly crispy. It is now ready to serve, but not before you add the grated parmesan and crushed black peppercorns.

Optional: Drizzle with extra virgin olive oil and balsamic vinegar. Mmmmm!

Serve and enjoy!

MINESTRONE SOUP

SERVES 2 OR 3

This is my take on minestrone soup. Yet again, I replace white potato with sweet potatoes. It really is a relaxed dish to which you can add your own ingredients if you wish. You can also vary the quantities of each ingredient to suit you. This meal is high in fibre.

INGREDIENTS

- **1 red onion, peeled and roughly chopped**
- **1 garlic clove, finely chopped**
- **1 large courgette, washed and cubed**
- **1 large sweet potato, peeled and chopped into cubes**
- **2 celery stalks, washed and cubed**
- **3 slim carrots, peeled and chopped**
- **400g small shaped pasta, preferably brown pasta.** I recommend the shapes farfalle (literally means little butterflies) or ditalini (very small tubes).
- **1/3 of a yellow/green cabbage, rinsed and shredded finely**
- **400g cannellini beans, drained**
- **400g chickpeas, drained**
- **2 vegetable stock cubes**
- **2 litres of water**
- **1 teaspoon of black pepper**
- **1 teaspoon of sea salt**
- **1 small handful of basil leaves, chopped**
- **1 teaspoon of dried oregano**
- **2 tablespoons of olive oil**

HOW TO MAKE:

Heat the oil in a large deep frying pan. Add the onion, garlic, celery, carrots and sweet potato. Fry for 5 minutes until the veg softens. Add the water to the pan, followed by the vegetable stock cubes. Once boiling, add the courgette, beans, chickpeas salt, pepper and cabbage. Cook for around 15 minutes, stirring occasionally.

Add the pasta, basil and oregano and cook for around 5-10minutes, until the pasta is al dente (the smaller the pasta, the quicker it will cook). When the pasta and sweet potato is cooked, it is ready to serve!

Optional: Serve with a side portion of rye or sourdough bread and sprinkle with parmesan or parmigiano cheese.

Serve in warm bowls and add another small sprinkle of black pepper.

MUSCLE ANATOMY

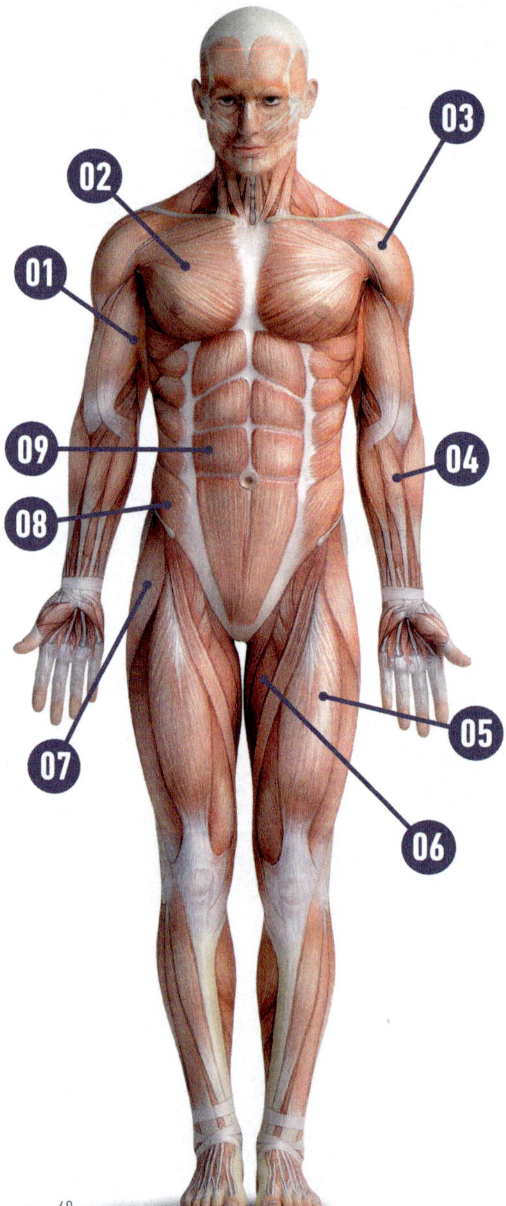

Although this book will concentrate on building your booty, it is useful to understand the other main muscle groups of your body. Some of them will be worked later in the book.

FRONT VIEW

01. Biceps brachii
(biceps)

02. Pectorals
(chest)

03. Deltoids
(shoulders)

04. Forearms

05. Quadriceps

06. Adductors
(hip flexors)

07. Abductors
(hip flexors)

08. Obliques

09. Rectus abdominis
(abdominal muscles; transverse abdominals are underneath the rectus abdominis)

REAR VIEW

10. Trapezius
11. Rhomboids
12. Triceps brachii
    (Triceps)
13. Latissimus dorsi
14. Erector spinae
    (lower back)
15. Gluteus medius
16. Gluteus maximus
    (gluteus minimus deeper behind)
17. Hamstrings
18. Calves

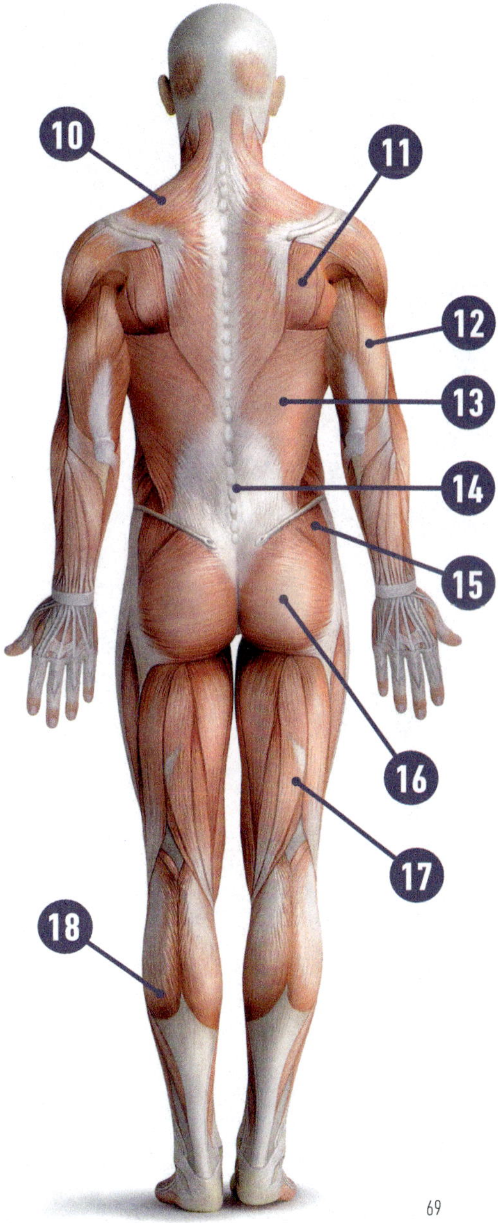

TRAINING & EXERCISE

NOW IT'S TIME FOR ACTION!

TRAINING & EXERCISE – NOW IT'S TIME FOR ACTION!

I've gone through lifestyle and nutrition, but now is the time to hit the gym with a training program I have designed for you. If you want to get your butt as big as its maximum potential, you will probably need to join a gym or attend tailored fitness classes, unless you are lucky enough to have your own gym at home.

FACT: Your mental health will benefit by setting goals and recording gains, which will boost your confidence and self-esteem.

TIP: If you are concerned about any health conditions you have, then it is very important you consult with a health professional before entering any exercise regime.

YOU MUST BE A BIG BELIEVER IN NO PAIN, NO GAIN!
If you are not prepared to sweat or ache the next day, you will fail!

I am not only going to provide you with a 38-session training program, but I am also going to list all the exercises that will help you see a change in your butt, and explain how to do them. I will also show you some of the abdominal/core strength exercises involved.

You won't see gains overnight. Sometimes it can take up to 10 weeks to see any change. But if you stick to the programme, you will notice the difference. People progress in different ways and at different rates. Some progress faster by increasing the weight-load (with the correct form) and others by performing more reps (with the correct form). And in squat exercises, some are able to squat lower than others (again, with the correct form).

Of course, there is nothing to stop you doing some other activities alongside the 38-session programme, such as running and yoga – in fact, I recommend it! There is more about the activities which particularly help you get your perfect booty towards the end of the book.

Before I get to the program, I will go through some important guidelines. These include a description of glute exercises (and the important warm-up and cool-down exercises), the repetition ranges, and training frequency. This will then be followed by the training programme.

But first I want to highlight the importance of breathing correctly during workouts.

We all know that breathing is important, right? Otherwise we would die! But as we are all human, we pick up bad habits!

BREATHING

Breathing ensures that the blood circulating to your working muscles is oxygenated. When lifting, it is important to breathe properly, not just for health reasons but it can also have a positive impact on physical performance.

So many of us (not intentionally) hold our breath whilst lifting weights. Or if not whilst lifting at the gym, whilst moving furniture or garden equipment. Improper breathing can lead to many problems, especially when lifting heavy items. One very important risk is that it can increase your blood pressure, which can lead to fainting or a heart attack. Other risks include fatigue and dizziness – not ideal when you have big booty goals! Correct breathing techniques have also been known to reduce recovery time between sets. Also, by breathing correctly when lifting, you will likely have a higher degree of control and alertness during your exercise.

The ideal technique is to not hold your breath during the exercise. Instead, exhale (breathe out) as you lift the weight and inhale (breathe in) as you lower the weight.

TIP: EXHALE as you lift the weight and INHALE as you lower the weight.

For example, if you were about to perform barbell squat. Ideally you should inhale as you begin to lower down, and exhale as you return to starting position.

Another example would be during conventional deadlift. Whilst performing the first set, inhale when you have grabbed the barbell at starting position. As you drive through with your hips and complete your first repetition, exhale.

Alternatively, on a non-booty exercise of push-ups (if your booty is having a rest but you are wanting to look after your upper body), inhale as you bend your elbows to lower your body down to the ground, and exhale as you rise back up.

On a bodyweight glute bridge, you inhale before the first repetition and exhale as you drive up with your hips. As your hips descend/return to the ground you then inhale again before you exhale as your hips go back up for the second repetition. This will all make more sense when you go through each exercise at a time in the coming pages.

TIP: If you struggle to get into the habit of breathing effectively (which is normal), then before you start a workout session, do some deep breathing exercises. Close your eyes and take in a deep breath through your nose, hold it for one or two seconds, then exhale through your mouth. Repeat this for a few minutes.

Practising this deep breathing before exercising enables you to improve your breathing during your workout. You may also find yourself more relaxed and more conscious of your breathing patterns.

As well as concentrating on your breathing, you should also pay attention to your core to avoid injury.

TIP: Engage your core by keeping the abdominal muscles tight whilst lifting!

HOW: As you breathe in (inhale), pull your belly/stomach all the way in and perform the exercise, whether it be squats, lunge, deadlift or any other lift!

FACT: By engaging your core and keeping the abdominal muscles tight, this decreases the possibility of sustaining an injury whilst exercising, especially if you are going to be lifting heavy!

FACT

Forcing your back into dangerous positions will put excessive pressure on your vertebrae and can lead to lumbar spondylosis.

Lumbar spondylosis is a form of lower back pain described as the degeneration of the lumbar vertebrae.

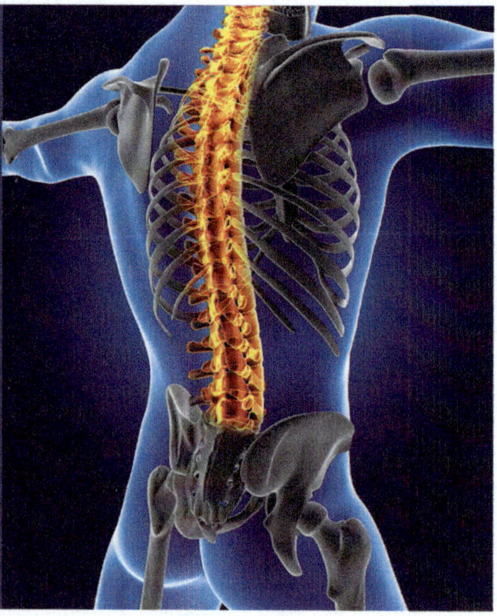

SQUATS

Squats are a popular compound exercise (works several parts of the body). The glutes are worked a great deal, but the quadriceps are the most worked in squats. It is a quad-dominant exercise and critical for preventing knee pain. Hamstrings are also a muscle group worked a lot in these exercises but not as much as the quadriceps. Surprisingly, your abdominal muscles also work as supportive muscles, so when you do a lot of squats the ab work builds up! The lower back and calves also play supportive roles. So these are a good all-rounder for the body.

Some people will be able to squat lower than others, some will be able to lift heavier weights than others – it's all down to your body. However, you will notice an improvement in your own performance over time.

FACT: Squats are fantastic for losing fat, especially cellulite!

In order to get a bigger butt, you will need to add weights after you perform the exercise correctly in bodyweight form.

BODYWEIGHT SQUAT

Muscles worked: glutes, quadriceps, hip flexors, hamstrings, calves, abdominals.

How: Stand with your feet shoulder-width apart. Either have your hands placed behind your head or out in front of you. Begin by flexing your knees and hips, sitting back using your hips as far as you can go without touching the floor. If possible, squat down to full depth (as low as you can go) then reverse the motion back to the starting position. Repeat for the desired amount of repetitions.

You may only get down a short way when you first start trying this exercise, but that is fine. It is all about improving week on week.

When you squat low, your hips and glutes take more of the weight. Squatting deeper requires more work from the muscles, especially from the posterior chain, which are the glutes, hamstrings and calves. Low squats also increase flexibility and stability in the lower back.

ADDING WEIGHT

Yep, in order to get big BOOTIEZ we need to add weight. There are many ways we can add weight to our squats.

BARBELL SQUAT

If you have not done this before, then practise with a light barbell or an empty barbell pole. You can either use a barbell from a rack of barbells that people use for other exercises such as bicep curls, or use the squat rack, which is ideal for progressing to heavier weights. Another option is the Smith machine, which people love or hate.

Using a squat rack – place the bar on the rack at chest height. Make sure you add weight evenly on both sides of the bar. Remember not to start heavy, especially if it is your first attempt. Lift up, placing your hands with a grip wider than shoulder width.

Muscles worked: glutes, quadriceps, hip flexors, hamstrings, calves, abdominals.

How: Begin with the barbell supported on top of the trapezius muscles (upper back). The chest should be up and the head facing forward. Have a hip-width stance.

Descend by flexing the knees, refraining from moving the hips back as much as possible. Your knees should travel forward but should not go further than your toes. Try to keep torso as upright as possible.

Continue all the way down until your upper legs contact your lower legs or go into a deeper squat. Reverse the motion, driving the weight upward.

SMITH MACHINE SQUAT

If you are doing this for the first time, get used to doing it with the correct technique and without any weight.

Make sure you set the bar appropriately so it is in line with your chest. Step underneath the bar and place the back of your shoulders across the bar. Choose your foot stance.

Muscles worked: glutes, quadriceps, hip flexors, hamstrings, calves, abdominals.

How: Grab on to the bar with both arms at each side of your body. Unlock the bar from the machine with your hands and lift it off the rack by pushing your legs and torso upwards and straight. Keep your head up and maintain a straight back. This is your starting position. Begin by slowly lowering the bar, bending the knees as you maintain a straight posture with the head up. Continue down until the angle between the upper leg and the calves becomes slightly less than 90-degrees so the upper legs are below parallel to the floor. Inhale as you perform this portion of the movement. The front of the knees should be above the toes but so that the knees are not past the toes. Return to starting position by raising the bar as you exhale by pushing the floor with your heel as you straighten the legs again back to the start. Repeat for the desired amount of repetitions.

DUMBBELL SQUAT

Many people choose to use dumbbells instead of a barbell. This could be if they feel uncomfortable having a barbell with heavy weight added. There could also be a long wait for the squat rack so they grab a pair of dumbbells to save time waiting around. This is an effective way to squat, yet slightly trickier to perform correctly. Practice!

Muscles worked: glutes, quadriceps, hip flexors, hamstrings, calves, abdominals.

How: Stand straight holding a dumbbell in each hand. Your palms should be facing the sides of your legs.

Position your legs using a shoulder-width medium stance with your toes pointed slightly out. Always keep your head up and avoid looking downwards. This is your starting position.

Begin to slowly lower your torso by bending your knees as you maintain a straight posture with the head up. Continue down until your knees are parallel to the floor.

Begin to raise your torso as you exhale by pushing the floor with the heel of your foot mainly as you straighten your legs and come back to the starting position. Repeat for the desired amount of repetitions you are aiming for.

Note: Due to the dumbbell being lower than hip height, you are less likely to go into a deeper squat than a barbell or goblet squat.

FACT: If your knees are further forward than that imaginary line past your toes, then you are placing undue stress on the knee and the exercise has been performed incorrectly.

FRONT BARBELL SQUAT

Although this does not target your glutes as much as the back barbell squat, some people prefer this method. They are able to squat slightly lower using this exercise and believe it is safer. Make sure you start with the barbell with little or no weight on it. You will not initially be able to squat with as much weight as the back barbell squat.

Muscles worked: glutes, quadriceps (greater extent), hip flexors, hamstrings (lower extent), calves, abdominals.

How: Set the bar on the rack so it best matches your height. The bar should sit comfortably across your trapezius muscles. Once the correct height is chosen and the bar is loaded, bring your arms up under the bar while keeping the elbows high and the upper arm slightly above parallel to the floor. Rest the bar on top of the deltoids. You can either use a cross-armed stance (arms crossed over like an X) or a standard arm stance.

Lift the bar off the rack by first pushing with your legs and straightening your torso.

Step away from the rack and position your legs using a shoulder-width medium stance and toes pointed slightly out. Keep your head up at all times and avoid looking downwards. Make sure you maintain a straight back. This is the starting position.

Begin to slowly lower the bar by bending the knees as you maintain a straight posture with the head up. Continue down until your upper legs are below parallel to the floor. Make sure you inhale in this part of the movement.

Begin to raise the bar as you exhale by pushing the floor mainly with the middle of your foot as you straighten the legs again and go back to the starting position. Repeat for the amount of repetitions you are aiming for.

GOBLET SQUAT

If you are new to squatting with weights, then this is a 'must' exercise. Easy, effective and can be performed with a kettlebell or dumbbell. However, as you become an 'intermediate' you can progress to heavier weights. To be honest, if you aren't ready to tackle the front barbell squat, this is a good way to build up to it as it works the lower body in a very similar way but is easier.

Muscles worked: glutes, quadriceps (greater extent), hip flexors, hamstrings (lower extent), calves, abdominals.

How: Stand holding a light kettlebell by the horns, close to your chest. If you are using a dumbbell, then cradle the head of the dumbbell close to your chest with both hands. You should be looking forward with shoulders back and your spine straight. Have your feet slightly wider than shoulder width. You can however adjust it to make it into a narrow-stance goblet squat or a sumo-stance goblet squat. This will be your starting position.

Whilst holding the dumbbell/kettlebell, squat down until your hamstrings are very close above your calves and briefly pause. Keep your chest and head up and your back straight.

At the bottom position, pause and use your elbows to push your knees out. Return to the starting position by extending the knees and hips and driving through your heels. Repeat for desired amount of repetitions.

VARIATIONS OF DIFFERENT SQUATS

Here are some variations on squats to keep it interesting and to work all parts of your lovely bums and give you attractive healthy legs as well!

FACT: Your foot stance alters how much/little each leg muscle is working during your squats!

TIP: If you really want bigger quads, use the front barbell squat technique and it will be a killer! By having a barbell on your front and a narrow foot position, it will be extra quad work so don't expect to be able to lift a heavy weight at first.

SUMO SQUAT

This places more emphasis on your inner thigh abductors as well as your glutes. This squat stance is becoming increasingly popular with bodybuilders and celebrities due to it targeting the inner thigh and gluteal muscles.

Muscles worked: glutes, quadriceps, hip flexors, hamstrings, abdominals, calves.

How: Have your feet wider than your shoulders and your toes slightly pointed out (imagine a sumo wrestler!). Slowly bend at the knees and drop your hips to lower your body, keeping your back straight . Repeat for the desired number of reps.

Progression: You need to add weight! Have a barbell placed across your back or hold a kettlebell in front of you as though you are doing a goblet squat. Execute the movement like you are doing the bodyweight version. And progress more by increasing the weight load. Repeat for the desired amount of repetitions.

SQUAT PULSE

This is a good exercise for building strength and definition.

Muscles worked: glutes, quadriceps, hip flexors, hamstrings, abdominals, calves.

How: Stand with your feet in squat starting position. Either have your arms out in front of you or in at your chest. Sit your ass back and lower into a squat. Keep your back straight, chest up and your core muscles in tight. Squat back up, but only so your hips are slightly higher than your knees. Then squat back down again so you feel the burn. Repeat for desired amount of repetitions.

Progression: Add weight! Have a barbell placed across your back or hold a kettlebell in front of you as though you are doing a goblet squat. Execute the movement like you are doing the bodyweight version. Progress more by increasing the weight load.

NARROW-LEGGED SQUAT

Whilst targeting the glutes, this exercise also targets the quadriceps to a greater extent.

Muscles worked: glutes, quadriceps (to a greater extent), hip flexor, hamstrings, abdominals, calves.

How: Have your stance slightly narrower than shoulder width. Slowly bend at the knees and drop your hips to lower your body, keeping your back straight. Repeat for the desired number of repetitions.

This squat should seem more difficult than a regular squat.

Progression: You need to add weight! Have a barbell placed across your back or add a dumbbell in each hand down at your sides. Or hold a kettlebell in front of you as though you are doing a goblet squat. Execute the movement as though you are doing the bodyweight version. And progress more by increasing the weight load.

WALKING SQUATS

This is slightly different to frog hops as you are not jumping, but it is tough and effective.

Muscles worked: glutes, quadriceps, hip flexors, hamstrings, calves, abdominals.

How: Have your feet at shoulder width. Get into a squat position and stay low whilst you walk forward. After a few steps or if you get to the other side of the room, turn around and squat walk back, or alternatively, repeat for the desired amount of repetitions.

Progression: I recommend adding a barbell across your back for this exercise to make it more challenging and booty sculpting. Using dumbbells would be very tricky, but could be done if you are up for the challenge!

HACK SQUAT

This involves a machine. You can adjust your feet in this exercise so they can be shoulder-width, narrower or wider. Not all gyms have this machine, so if you need to replace this, I recommend doing the dumbbell, Smith machine or barbell squat instead.

Muscles worked: glutes, quadriceps, hip flexors, hamstrings, calves, abdominals.

How: Position your back and shoulders against the pad of the machine with your feet on the platform at shoulder width. This will be your starting position.

While keeping your head and eyes up and back straight, squat until your upper thighs are parallel to the floor. Breathe in as you slowly go down. Pressing mainly with the heel of the foot and squeezing the thighs, go back up as you breathe out. Repeat for the desired amount of repetitions.

Progression: Add weight plates on both sides of the bars at the sides of the hack squat machine.

FROG HOPS

This is another good contractual exercise, like the squat pulse. An enjoyable and effective exercise.

Muscles worked: glutes, quadriceps, hip flexors, hamstrings, calves, abdominals.

How: Stand with your hands behind your head and squat down, keeping your head up, back straight and core tight. Jump forward several feet, avoiding jumping unnecessarily high. As your feet contact the ground, absorb the impact through your legs and jump again. Repeat for the desired number of repetitions.

BULGARIAN SPLIT SQUAT

Like the single-legged squat, a great squat for balance, hip mobility and single-legged strength. This is a more intense squat so there is no need to add weight until your strength has increased a lot due to training. If you love a challenge, this is the one for you and your glutes!

Muscles worked: glutes, quadriceps, hip flexors, hamstrings, calves, abdominals.

How: Stand with your back facing a bench or a box of equal height. Reach one foot back and place that foot on top of the box or bench. Lower your back knee down towards the ground by bending your front leg. When the front leg is parallel to the ground, return to the start of the move by using your grounded foot and hips. Repeat for the desired number of repetitions.

Progression: It is very popular to add a barbell across your traps/back despite already being a challenging exercise when done as bodyweight form. Alternatively, hold a kettlebell in front of you or hold two dumbbells, one at each side of you.

SINGLE-LEG SQUAT

This is a vital exercise as it is fantastic for single leg strength as well as increased use of balancing muscles, including abdominals. Also, it provides increased resistance.

Muscles worked: glutes, quadriceps, hamstrings, hip flexors, abdominals, calves.

How: Begin by having your arms extended out in front of you or behind your head. Balance on one leg with your opposite leg out in front of you, keep your core engaged and stay rooted on the grounded foot.

Squat down as far as possible, keeping your elevated foot off the floor. Squat back up to the starting position until your grounded leg is straight. Repeat for the desired amount of repetitions.

Progression: Add weight! Have a barbell placed across your back or hold a kettlebell in front of you as though you are doing a goblet squat. Execute the movement like you are doing the bodyweight version. Progress more by increasing the weight load.

BENCH/BOX SQUAT

The box squat allows you to squat to a desired depth and develop explosive gluteal and leg strength in the squat movement. I think this is extremely underrated and underused as an exercise. You can increase the intensity by using a lower bench/box. You are really engaging your glutes to squat back up off the box after squatting down onto it.

Muscles worked: glutes, quadriceps, hip flexors, hamstrings, calves, abdominals.

How: Begin with a box at the appropriate height behind you. Typically, you should aim for a box height that brings you to a squat so your hips are slightly lower than your knees. But you can train higher or lower if desired.

Adjust your feet wider for more emphasis on the back, glutes, adductors and hamstrings, or closer together for more quad development. If you are doing this bodyweight, have your arms out in front of you or folded with hands on opposite shoulders and your head facing forward.

With your back, shoulders and core tight, push your knees and butt out and begin your descent. Sit back with your hips until you are seated on the box. Ideally, your shins should be perpendicular to the ground. Pause when you reach the box and relax the hip flexors. Never bounce off the box/bench.

Keeping the weight on your heels and pushing your feet and knees out, drive upward off the box as you lead the movement with your head. Continue upward, maintaining tightness head to toe. Repeat for the desired number of repetitions.

Progression: Yep, go big or go home! Add a barbell across your upper back and you will make your ass work super hard when you lift it up and off the box. Alternatively, hold a dumbbell or kettlebell as though you would while doing a goblet squat.

WALL SQUAT

Another killer. Make sure you inhale and exhale continuously throughout this exercise.

Muscles worked: glutes, quadriceps, hip flexors, hamstrings, calves, abdominals.

How: Begin with your back against the wall and have your feet approximately 20 inches out in front of you. Have your feet in a shoulder-width stance, and your toes and knees pointed slightly out. This is the starting position.

Lower your body by sliding down the wall, keeping your head up and maintaining a flat back against the wall. Continue until your upper legs are just below parallel to the floor. Maintain this position for your desired amount of time.

Push through your heels to return back up to starting position. Repeat for the desired number of repetitions.

Progression: Hold a kettlebell in front of your chest – but believe me, you are unlikely to add anywhere as much weight as you would for a regular type of squat!

SIDE-WALKING SQUAT

A variation of the side squat walk.

Muscles worked: glutes, quadriceps, hip flexors, hamstrings, calves, abdominals.

How: Squat down, feet shoulder-width apart. Step aside with one leg to widen your position whilst in squat mode. Then bring in the opposite leg so you are back with your feet at shoulder width. Keep doing it until you have side-walked to the other side of the room or alternatively, repeat for the desired number of repetitions.

Progression: I recommend adding a barbell across your back for this exercise to make it more challenging and booty sculpting. Or hold a kettlebell in front of you.

DUMBBELL BETWEEN PLATFORM SQUAT

This exercise is trending more and more due to the wide range of motion used by the hips and the extra deep squat involved. Your glutes are also targeted really well, especially if you engage them when you squat back up. Alternatively, you can use a kettlebell (as pictured) instead of a dumbell.

Set up: Set platforms so that when you stand on them with one foot on each platform, your feet are shoulder-width apart. Place the dumbbell between the platforms.

Muscles worked: glutes, quadriceps, hip flexors, hamstrings, calves, abdominals.

How: Grab a dumbbell with both hands underneath the top bell. Your arms should be straight and in front of your groin and the dumbbell should be between your legs. Get on the platforms, standing with your feet shoulder-width apart. Either have your toes pointed forward or slightly out to the side.

Keep your chest tall and squat right down until your hip joints are beneath your knees. Make sure you are also bending at the knees throughout the duration of the movement.

Push back up with your heels and also engage your glutes so you feel the burn. Repeat for the desired amount of reps.

Progression: Increase the weight by using a heavier dumbbell or kettlebell.

KEEP IT UP!

ARE YOU READY FOR HIP THRUSTS?

GLUTE BRIDGES AND HIP THRUSTS

These exercises are perfect and extremely important for building/sculpting the butt of your dreams. The gluteus maximus takes up more slack in these exercises than in squats, lunges and deadlifts. The question is why? Because these bootylicous exercises strengthen the glutes through a full range of motion!

Also, by doing these exercises often it will strengthen your bum. And therefore allow you to increase the weight load and better the appearance of that backside. Not only that, these exercises can be so much fun as they are slightly provocative!

FACT: Glute-dominant exercises help people from suffering lower back pain by teaching the body to engage the glutes during hip dominant exercises rather than putting excessive pressure on the lower back.

GLUTE BRIDGE

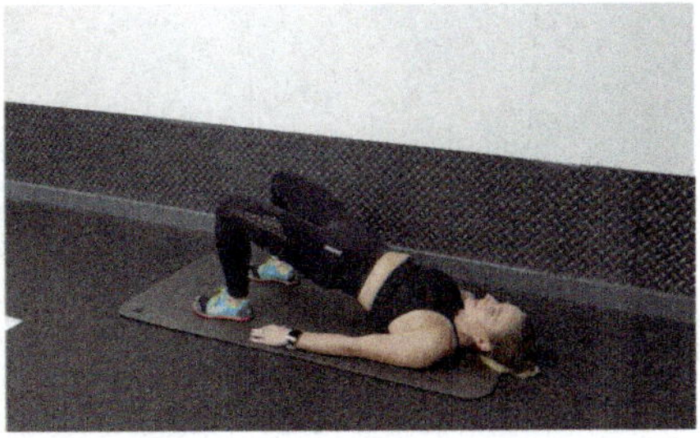

The bodyweight glute bridge is easy and effective for beginners. Of course, you will need to add weight sooner rather than later as you train in order to see booty gains!

Muscles worked: glutes (especially gluteus maximus), hamstrings, hip flexors, abdominals.

How: Lie facing up on the floor with your knees bent and your feet flat on the ground. Keep your arms at your side with your palms down.

Pushing mainly with your heels, lift your hips off the floor while keeping your back straight. Breathe out as you perform this part of the motion and hold at the top for a second.

Slowly go back to the starting position as you breathe in. Repeat for the desired amount of repetitions.

GLUTE BRIDGE HOLD

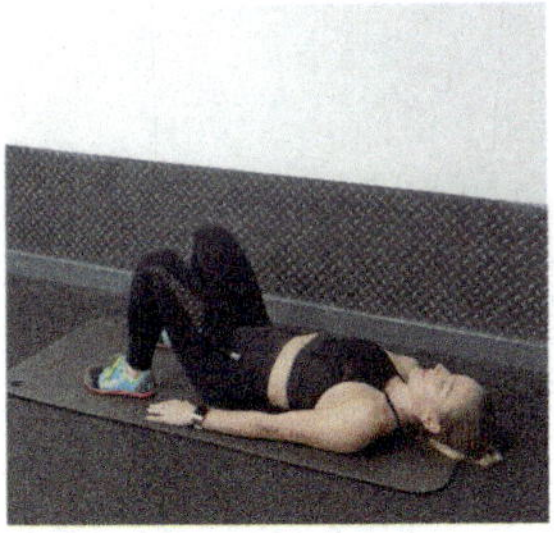

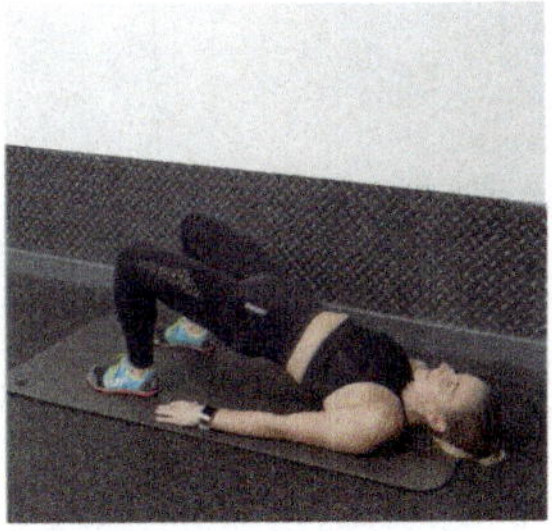

This is an exercise that is harder than it looks because you are holding your hips and glutes up and squeezing with your hips and glutes.

Muscles worked: glutes (especially gluteus maximus), hamstrings, hip flexors, abdominals.

How: Lie on the floor with your knees bent and feet flat on the ground. Lift your hips off the ground so you are in glute bridge position. Hold the bridged position for 15 seconds or until you feel the burn!

Progression: Whilst in glute bridge, after doing the desired amount of reps, lower your hips down an inch or two then raise them back up and repeat for the desired amount of reps. This is known as glute bridge pulse.

Alternatively, drop your hips down an inch or two and raise one hip up and repeat with the other hip. This way you are isolating each butt cheek!

ONE-LEGGED GLUTE BRIDGE

This is a good way to progress if you are exercising at home and you don't have any weights. You are involving single leg/glute/hip strength too. It's surprisingly challenging without the use of any equipment!

Muscles worked: glutes (especially gluteus maximus), hamstrings, hip flexors, abdominals.

How: Lie on the floor with your feet flat and knees bent. Raise one leg off of the ground, this will be your starting position. Execute the movement by driving through the heel, extending your hip upward and raising your glutes off the ground. Repeat for the desired amount of repetitions.

Progression: Why not add the 15-second glute bridge hold by using just one leg to hold? Or add the pulse option with just one leg/ass cheek? Or do both!

INCLINE GLUTE BRIDGE

Doing this bodyweight exercise involves a greater deal of gluteal and hamstring strength compared to the regular glute bridge as it involves more movement from the muscles.

Muscles worked: glutes (especially gluteus maximus), hamstrings (greater extent), abdominals.

How: Lie on the floor with your buttocks and lower back on the floor and your heels on a bench/box/platform. Execute by lifting your hips up as high as you can.

Progression: You can progress by using just one leg.

CALF-RAISED GLUTE BRIDGE

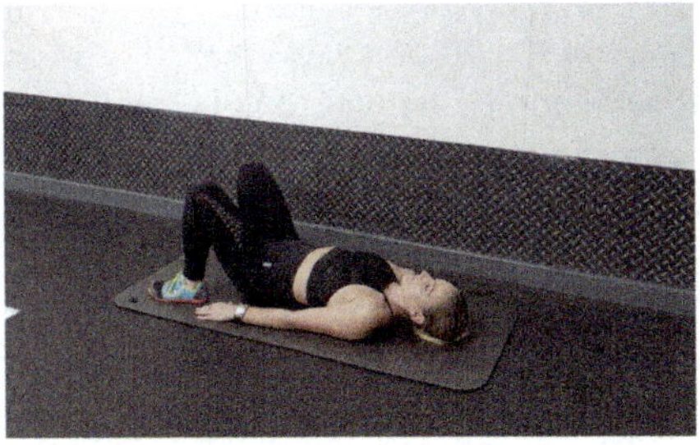

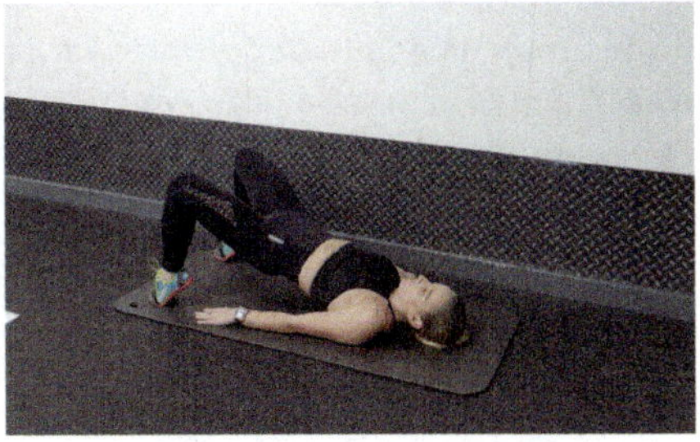

Why not add a bit of calf work? Doing this also means you are holding the glute bridge for even longer. After a few reps you will be feeling it in your calves AND glutes!

Muscles worked: calves, glutes (especially gluteus maximus), hamstrings, abdominals.

How: Perform standard glute bridge. As your hips go up, hold and raise your heels off the ground and hold for a second or two. Repeat for desired amount of reps.

Progression: It's difficult to add weight to this type of glute bridge. But you could always add the glute bridge hold.

TIP: Do 10-15 glute bridges then a 15-second glute bridge hold or longer. You'll feel it!

ADDING WEIGHT TO GLUTE BRIDGE VARIATIONS

Glute bridge is a fantastic way to work and isolate the buttocks, but if you want them to grow and grow, you need to add weight. Using a barbell is the recommended way of adding weight. However, some people prefer to use dumbbells instead.

Use a barbell with no added weight if it's your first time.

If you are ready to add weight to the barbell, there are 2 options to get the barbell into position. Most 20kg weight plates are large enough for you to roll the barbell up over your legs and into position over your hips and into starting position.

Alternatively, ask a fitness instructor or training partner to lift the barbell in and out of position over your hips. Using the partner method is dangerous if you are using 40kg or more.

BARBELL GLUTE BRIDGE

A fantastic exercise for using and progressing to very heavy weights, this can only lead to BIG booty gains!

Muscles worked: glutes (especially gluteus maximus), hamstrings, abdominals.

Setup: Lie on the floor with your legs out on the floor. Once the barbell is in place over your hips, adjust your legs so you are in glute bridge starting position.

How: Begin the movement by pushing through with your heels, extending your hips towards the ceiling. Extend as far as possible and hold for a couple of seconds, then reverse the motion to return to the starting position. Repeat for the desired amount of reps.

Progression: Once your hips are fully extended upwards, hold for up to 5 seconds per rep. Trust me, you'll feel it! Progress further by adding weight.

DUMBBELL GLUTE BRIDGE

No matter how much padding is on the barbell, some people still find it uncomfortable. Some dumbbells are not suitable as they are made up with thin weight plates which will dig into your hips and cause discomfort.

Some dumbbells are perfect for glute bridge exercises. For example, if they have rubber padding around the dumbbell and it is not pressing too hard into your hip. Normally, you will not be able to lift with as much weight as you would with a barbell, but that doesn't say you can't smash gains!

Muscles worked: glutes (especially gluteus maximus), hamstrings, abdominals.

You will still need an instructor to lift it onto your hips, but it must be done with caution, especially if it is a heavier weight. A lighter weighted dumbbell (such as 15kg) could be lifted onto your hips yourself. For safety, place your hands on the top of the dumbbell so you are keeping the dumbbell stationary and the dumbbell does not roll onto your chest or face.

How: Begin the movement by pushing through with your heels, extending your hips towards the ceiling. Extend as far as possible and hold for a couple of seconds, then reverse the motion to return to the starting position. Repeat for the desired amount of reps.

Progression: Once your hips are fully extended upwards, hold for 5 seconds per rep. Also, progress by using a heavier dumbbell.

HIP THRUSTS

Hip thrusts have got a similar reputation to the glute bridge for being a 'platinum' glute-building exercise. The hips move through a good range of motion and the glutes provide a lot of physical force in this exercise. There is a lot more movement and range of motion in the hip thrust than there is in the glute bridge.

You will need a padded training bench for this exercise so it is comfy for your back. Whatever you do, do not substitute a training bench for anything with rough or sharp edges!

Setup: Position a flat bench in an open space and secure it with something heavy to prevent it sliding forwards. Sit straight-legged on the floor with your upper-back resting on the bench. Have your feet at approximately shoulder-width apart. Make sure you have enough of your back on the bench so you do not slide off.

BODYWEIGHT HIP THRUST

Muscles worked: glutes (especially gluteus maximus), hamstrings, abdominals.

How: Drive your hips up towards the ceiling, pushing through your heels and squeezing your glutes. Keep knees in line with your toes. Whilst in top position, your hips should be fully extended and your torso should be parallel to the floor. Pause for 2 seconds as you are squeezing the glutes – oh yeah! Lower your hips down towards the floor so you are back into starting position. Repeat for the desired number of reps.

Progression: Add the hip thrust hold option just like you'd be doing in glute bridge hold. After the last repetition, hold at the top of the movement for 15 seconds. Or add the pulse option as well!

Adding weight: Like glute bridge, you add a barbell or a dumbbell to see BIG results.

Using a barbell, load it evenly each side. Sit straight-legged on the floor with your upper body resting on the bench. Either carefully roll the barbell over your legs or get a trainer or gym partner to do it for you. If the combined weight is more than 40kg, ask someone to lift the barbell and place it over your hips.

BARBELL HIP THRUST

This is where we mean business! Lots of opportunity to progress to lots of added weight and make your glutes use force. And see results!

Muscles worked: glutes (especially gluteus maximus), hamstrings, abdominals.

How: Once the barbell is positioned on your hips, drive your hips up towards the ceiling, pushing through your heels and squeezing your glutes. Keep knees in line with your toes.

Whilst in top position, your hips should be fully extended and your torso should be parallel to the floor. Pause for 2 seconds as you are squeezing the glutes.

Progression: Again, why not hold for 5 seconds per rep? Even 'The Rock' recommends doing this!

DUMBBELL HIP THRUST

If you are using a heavy dumbbell, you will need an instructor to lift it onto your hips. However, use with caution, especially if of a heavier weight. Throughout the exercise, place your hands in a way so that the dumbbell doesn't rock to the side and/or cause discomfort.

Muscles worked: glutes (especially gluteus maximus), hamstrings, abdominals.

How: Drive your hips up towards the ceiling, pushing through your heels and squeezing your glutes. Keep knees in line with your toes.

Whilst in top position, your hips should be fully extended and your torso should be parallel to the floor. Pause for 2 seconds as you are squeezing the glutes.

Progression: Again, why not hold for 5 seconds per rep? Even I recommend doing this! Lol!

CRAB HIP THRUST

This bodyweight exercise will work your arms and your core will be more engaged. This can be done anywhere with no equipment needed and is surprisingly challenging and effective!

Muscles worked: glutes (especially gluteus maximus), hamstrings, abdominals, triceps.

How: First sit on the floor with your legs out and seated up with your hands behind past your glutes and shoulders. Then bend your knees and tuck your feet in so that your feet are in line with your knees and shoulder-width apart, with your feet flat on the floor. Drive your hips up towards the ceiling, pushing through your heels and squeezing your glutes. Bring your hips down to the starting position and repeat for desired amount of reps.

Progression: Add a 15-second hold on the last repetition at the top of the movement. And/or add a few pulses. You will be making your core and triceps work very hard, as well as your sexy booty!

THRUSTERS OFF THE BOX

This is also a great bodyweight form of hip thrust as it allows a brilliant range of motion. For this you will need to place a box and a bench close enough together so your back can be on the bench and your feet up on the box with your knees bent roughly to about 90 degrees.

Muscles worked: glutes (especially gluteus maximus), hamstrings, abdominals.

How: Place your upper back on the bench and your heels up on the box. Drive up through your heels, glutes and upper back by engaging these muscles and then press up your hips and squeeze your glutes! Once you have lifted your hips to full extension, hold for a second or two then lower back down. Your beautiful ass should go lower than the box and bench. Repeat for desired number of reps.

Progression: Add a 15-second hold on the last repetition at the top of the movement. And/or add a few pulses.

LUNGES

Lunges are lower body compound (several muscle groups worked) exercises, like squats, that especially target the quads.

Certain types of lunges really target the glutes. With the reverse lunge and walking lunge you are putting extra work on the gluteus maximus and medius as you use these muscles to lift off and balance. With lateral lunge, you are using more of the gluteus medius and minimus muscles.

FORWARD BODYWEIGHT LUNGE

This lunge puts more work on the quadriceps than any other muscle, but still works glutes. As it mainly works the quadriceps, we normally only use this exercise for warming up.

Muscles worked: glutes, quadriceps (greater extent), hip flexors, hamstrings, calves, abdominals.

How: Stand still with your feet hip-width apart, chest out, and shoulders back, maintaining the natural curvature of your spine. Your knees should be unlocked and your hands on your hips.

Then take a moderate-length step forward with one foot, descending to a point at which your rear knee approaches the floor without touching, maintaining your body's upright posture. Your front knee should bend approximately 90 degrees, but for the sake of your knees, it should not be forward of the vertical plane that extends straight up from your toes. Take a slightly longer step if you need.

From the bottom position, push back up from your forward foot, bringing it back beside the other into starting position.

Either repeat on the same leg or the opposite side for the required number of repetitions.

Progression: You need to add weight! Have a barbell placed across your back or add a dumbbell in each hand down at your sides. Execute the movement as though you are doing the bodyweight version. And progress more by increasing the weight load.

BACKWARDS BODYWEIGHT LUNGE

This lunge targets the glutes a lot more than the forward lunge. During the training programme we will be doing a lot more of this type of lunge. But before you add weight, this must be mastered in the correct form before you add a barbell or dumbbells.

Muscles worked: glutes, quadriceps, hip flexors, hamstrings, abdominals, calves.

How: Begin in a standing position. Your hands should be on your hips or hanging at your sides. Look directly forward, keeping your chest up, with your feet shoulder-width apart. This will be your starting position.

Start the movement by taking a step back, bend your front knee so it's at a 90-degree angle and lower your other knee until it nearly touches the ground using a slow and controlled motion. The front knee should stay in line with the foot, and your upper body should remain neutral.

After a brief pause, return to the starting position by driving through the heel of the front leg to extend the knees and hips, and stepping forward with your back knee so you return to starting position.

This movement can be done completely on one side before switching, or can be performed in an alternating fashion.

Progression: You need to add weight. Have a barbell placed across your back or add a dumbbell in each hand down at your sides. Execute the movement as though you are doing the bodyweight version. And progress more by increasing the weight load.

STATIONARY LUNGE

This is my favourite type of lunge as I feel like I am doing a lot of work on one leg in a short space of time before I move onto the other leg. This is due to not including the step backwards and forwards as on the forwards and backwards lunge.

I feel a lot more burn and it is an exercise which increases balance and core strength.

Muscles worked: glutes, quadriceps, hip flexors, hamstrings, abdominals, calves.

How: Stand tall with your feet hip-distance apart then take a large step backward with one foot. This is your start position.

Lower the back knee to a 90-degree angle so both knees are bent, then press up to start position and repeat. After desired number of reps, switch legs/side.

Progression: Again, you need to add weight. Have a barbell placed across your back or add a dumbbell in each hand down at your sides.

Execute the movement as though you are doing the bodyweight version. Progress further by increasing the weight load. My preference is the dumbbell option as it is a lot more comfortable and easier to balance on this type of lunge.

LUNGE WALKS

Although you are lunging forwards, this has a reputation as a booty burner due to the large stretch load it induces on the glutes. It's also a more refreshing type of lunge as you are moving forwards from one end of the room to another.

Muscles worked: glutes, quadriceps, hip flexors, hamstrings, abdominals, calves.

How: Start by standing with your feet shoulder-width apart with your hands on your hips. Step forward with one leg, flexing the knees to drop your hips. Lunge downwards until your rear knee nearly touches the ground. Your posture should remain upright and your front knee should stay above the front foot.

Drive through the heel of your lead foot and extend both knees to raise yourself back up.

Step forward with your rear foot, repeating the lunge on the opposite leg. Repeat for the desired number of reps.

Progression: You can add weight to the walking lunge by placing a barbell across your back or by having a dumbbell at each side of you. However, avoid adding too much weight as it will be more difficult with the weight load than the other lunges.

Another option which will go nicely with the walking lunge is to hold a kettlebell or weight plate in front of you, holding it as if you are doing the goblet squat.

BULGARIAN SPLIT SQUAT

Yes I know I have already included this in squats, but many people believe it is a lunge although it says squat. Whether you say squat or lunge - it works your ass and legs hard enough to make you oooh!

Muscles worked: glutes, quadriceps, hip flexors, hamstrings, calves, abdominals.

How: Stand with your back facing a bench or a box of equal height. Reach one foot back and place the foot on top of the box or bench. Lower your back knee down towards the ground by bending your front leg. When the front leg is parallel to the ground, return to the start of the move by using your grounded foot and hips.

Progression: Add a barbell across the back or hold a dumbbell at each side of you. Or you could hold a dumbbell or kettlebell as if you were doing goblet squats.

LATERAL LUNGE

Another lunge that targets the gluteus medius and minimus. This is a more unusual type of lunge so it's refreshing but takes time to get used to.

Muscles worked: glutes, quadriceps, inner thighs, hip flexors, hamstrings, calves, abdominals.

How: Stand erect with your feet about shoulder-width apart. Your chest should be out, shoulders back, and knees unlocked. Maintain the natural curvature in your back. This is your start position. Facing forward throughout and staying as upright as possible, take a big step out to your side, angling your foot just slightly out. Descend into a moderately deep squat, keeping your trailing leg straight. Push back up and bring your leg back to the start position. Repeat on the opposite side and complete the desired number of repetitions.

Progression: You can add a pair of dumbbells at each side of you (I normally choose this option), or a barbell across your back. Or you can hold a kettlebell in front of you, holding it as though you were doing goblet squat.

CURTSY LUNGE

This is a very good exercise for targeting your inner thighs and your gluteus medius and minimus, which are often missed out in many lower body exercises.

Muscles worked: glutes (gluteus medius and minimus to a greater extent), quadriceps, inner thighs, hip flexors, hamstrings, calves, abdominals.

How: Stand with your feet shoulder-width apart. You should be looking straight forward with your chest up and shoulders back. This will be your starting position.

Initiate the movement by shifting your weight to your right foot, lifting your left from the ground. While keeping your torso facing forward, place your left leg behind your right, taking a wide, lateral step so it goes behind the front leg.

Descend into a lunge by bending your knees, lowering your body straight down. Continue until your front knee is at approximately 90 degrees, and then drive through the heel and extend the knee and hip.

As you come back up, return the back leg to the starting position. Complete by switching back and forth between both sides for the desired number of repetitions.

Progression: Add weight by holding a kettlebell at waist height in front of you as you do in a goblet squat. Alternatively, you could add a barbell across your back or a dumbbell at each side of you.

DEADLIFTS

Many people say squats and deadlifts are very similar, and to a certain extent it is true. In squats, the knees bend a lot and the quads are one of the main muscles used. In deadlifts, quadriceps are worked to a lesser degree, knees are more straightened and the hamstrings are worked to a greater degree. The deadlift is a hip dominant exercise.

You are normally able to lift heavier in deadlifts than you are in squats as more muscle groups are used. The movement in deadlift is centred mainly on the hip joint. More importantly, glutes are worked hard and your hips are strengthened a great deal. Strong hips help strong BOOTIEZ!

TIP: Posture differences between squats and deadlifts: Hips stay a lot higher in deadlifts.

CHOOSE WHICH GRIP IS BEST FOR YOU

Double overhand grip (pronated grip): This is considered a classic way to hold the barbell with both palms facing you. This is a convenient grip to get a good grip. However, as you progress with the weight, this grip is considered a limiting factor when you deadlift as the grip strength becomes weaker.

Mixed grip: This is when you alternate by having one hand grabbing with an overhand grip and the other with and underhand. Many people believe that this grip makes it a lot harder for the barbell to roll forward out of your hands.

My opinion: Start with the overhand grip. As you progress with the weight but struggle with the grip, switch to the mixed grip and you may realise that your grip was holding you back, not your strength!

STANDARD/CONVENTIONAL DEADLIFT

I love this exercise as it burns so many parts of the body, and really burns your glutes, lower body and also your lower back. Your entire posterior chain – lats, arms, deltoids, rhomboids and trapezius muscles – are also worked. This exercise will do wonders for lean muscle, strength and improvements in athleticism.

Muscles worked: Almost all over body. Glutes, hamstrings, arms, trapezius, lower back, shoulders, abdominals.

How: Start by standing in a narrow stance with your feet pointing straight and your shins approximately 2 inches from the barbell. Sit back and downwards. Bend over and grab hold of the barbell, ensuring you keep an even grip. You can use a double overhand grip (pronated grip) or a mixed grip.

In order to go heavy, you will need to use a mixed hand grip (one hand over and one under). However, like all exercises, if it's your first time, then start by using just the barbell. If you are using a lighter load, then a double overhand grip can be used.

Keep your chest up and hold a strong lower back arch. Your hips should be higher than your knees, and your shoulders should be higher than your hips. Your shoulders should be just slightly in front of the bar.

Just before you lift, make sure your neck is in a neutral position. Inhale, then exhale and raise the barbell. Throughout the repetition, the bar should be skimming your body (slightly touching). During this, your lower body will want to round and your pelvis will want to roll rearwards. Please don't allow this to happen!

As you rise to full extension so you are stood tall, use your sexy glutes to push your sexy hips forward to lockout. When you are going back down, begin by sitting backwards, keeping a strong lower back arch.

Progression: Increase the weight. Alternatively, hold a dumbbell in each arm at each side of your body as if you were holding a kettle. Hold the left dumbbell at a 5 or 10 past the clock angle and the right dumbbell at a 5 or 10 to the clock angle.

STIFF-LEGGED DEADLIFT

This is a unique deadlift as it is known to be more of a glutes and hamstring isolation type of deadlift, yet allows you to train heavy.

Muscles worked: glutes, hamstrings, lower back, abdominals.

How: Stand with your torso straight and your legs spaced using a shoulder-width or narrower stance. The knees should be slightly bent. This is your starting position.

Hold a bar using an overhand grip and your palms facing down. You may need to add wrist wraps if using a significant amount of weight. Keeping the knees stationary, lower the barbell to over the top of your feet by bending at the waist while keeping your back straight. Keep moving forward as if you are going to pick something up from the floor. You should feel a stretch on the hamstrings. Inhale as you perform this movement. Start bringing your torso up straight again by extending your hips until you are back at the starting position. Exhale as you perform this movement.

Repeat for the recommended amount of repetitions.

Please note, the back will normally be rounded at the bottom of the movement so avoid using excess weight.

Progression: Increase the weight. Alternatively, replace the barbell with dumbbells in each hand directly in front of your quadriceps.

ROMANIAN DEADLIFT

This is very good for targeting your hamstrings whilst still doing a great amount of work to your glutes.

Muscles worked: glutes, hamstrings, lower back, abdominals.

How: Stand holding a bar with your feet hip-width apart and the bar at hip level with palms facing down as you grip (overhand grip). Keep shoulders back and knees slightly bent.

Lower the bar by moving your glutes back as far as you can whilst keeping the bar close to your body and your head forwards. Your shoulders should also remain back. Try to reach the maximum range of your hamstring flexibility so you take the bar just below the knee if possible. Avoid any further movement afterwards.

At the bottom of your range of motion, return to starting position using your hips to drive forward.

Repeat for desired amount of repetitions.

Progression: Increase the weight. Alternatively, replace the barbell with dumbbells in each hand directly in front of your quadriceps.

THE DIFFERENCE BETWEEN STIFF-LEGGED AND ROMANIAN DEADLIFT?

On the Romanian deadlift, you push your hips back so the bar is as close as possible to your body at all times. When the bar is just past your knees, you quickly straighten your legs back, driving through with your hips. The bar is lowered as low as the lifter can go without rounding the back.

In Stiff-legged deadlift, the bar goes a lot lower, the hips stay locked and the hips don't move. The back is rounded at the bottom of the movement.

TIP: If you have back problems, then the Romanian deadlift is more suitable for you.

SUMO DEADLIFT

My favourite deadlift! On this deadlift, you are doing less work on your lower back and doing more work on your quads, inner thigh and your BOOTY! This, in my opinion, is by far the safest to lift heavy – though, of course, don't go so heavy that you can't posture correctly.

Muscles worked: lower back, quadriceps, glutes, hamstrings, hip flexors.

How: Begin with a bar loaded on the ground. Approach the bar so that it intersects the point directly in the middle between your feet. Your feet should be set very wide, so they are close to the weight plates of the bar. Bend at the hips to grip the bar. Your arms should be directly below the shoulders, inside your legs, and you can use a pronated grip or a mixed grip. Relax the shoulders, which should lengthen your arms.

Take a breath, and then lower your hips, looking forward, with your head and your chest up. Drive through the floor, spreading your feet apart, with your weight on the back half of your feet. Extend through the hips and knees.

As the bar passes through the knees, lean back and drive the hips into the bar.

Return the weight to the ground by bending at the hips and controlling the weight on the way down.

Progression: Increase the weight. Alternatively, use a kettlebell and hold it in front of you with both hands. Though it is extremely unlikely you will be able to progress the weight as if you were using a barbell.

TIP: Choose which grip is best for you.

INDIVIDUAL EXERCISES

HYPEREXTENSION/BACK EXTENSIONS

These exercises are underrated and unique in their benefit when they are done effectively. Despite being known for being a lower back exercise, it really targets the glutes at the top of the movement and the hamstrings at the bottom. However, you would need to make sure the exercise is done correctly as it is quite a technical exercise to execute – so pay close attention!

Muscles worked: glutes, hamstrings, lower back, hip flexors.

How: Lie face down on a hyperextension bench, tucking your ankles securely under the footpads. Adjust the upper pad if possible so your upper thighs lie flat across the wide pad, leaving enough room for you to bend at the waist without any restriction.

With your body straight, cross your arms in front of you (my preference) or behind your head. This will be your starting position.

Start bending forward slowly at the waist as far as you can while keeping your back flat. Inhale as you perform this movement. Keep moving forward until you feel a nice stretch on the hamstrings and you can no longer keep going without rounding your back. Slowly raise your torso back to the initial position as you exhale. Repeat for the recommended amount of repetitions.

Progression: Add some weight! You can hold a weight plate for extra resistance in front of you under your crossed arms. Another option is to hold a dumbbell with both hands close to your chest.

TIP: Never round the back as you perform this exercise. Ideally you go as far as your body allows you to without rounding the back.

LEG PRESS

This exercise is a very effective compound exercise but it requires a lot of setup.

Set up: Load the weight plates onto the machine and set the safety stop in the right position for your range of motion. Seat yourself at the machine, place your legs on the platform and choose your foot stance.

WHERE SHOULD I PLACE MY FEET ON THE PLATFORM?

All the feet positions target your legs, but each one activates a certain leg area.

High foot placement – targets your upper hamstrings and glutes. It increases the degree of hip extension and flexion whilst reducing the range of motion of the knees. In my opinion, this is a fantastic and underrated method to boost glute growth and strength!

Low foot placement – gives more work to your quadriceps and less on glutes and hamstrings. This is because there's more range of motion around the knees.

Basic stance placement – your feet shoulder-width apart. This is for overall leg development and will target all areas.

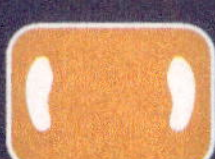

Wide foot placement – works the inner quad/thigh muscles. This is similar to doing a sumo squat.

Narrow foot placement – targets your outer quad/thigh muscles. If you really want to boost your quadriceps, combine the lower stance and narrow stance together.

Grip the handles at the side of the seat firmly. Straighten your legs to take the weight off the racks. Certain leg press machines will automatically unlock the safety mechanism after you straighten your legs. On others, you will need to manually release it. Your knees should still be slightly bent, however. This is the starting position for each rep.

Muscles worked: quadriceps, glutes, hamstrings, calves, hip abductors.

How: Start by inhaling, then lowering your legs to bring your knees in towards your chest. Don't allow your heels to lift off the platform or your booty to lift out of the seat. Pause for a moment in the bottom position, keeping tension in your legs. Exhale and push with your heels and your legs to return to the starting position. Repeat for the required number of reps.

Progression: Increase the weight! If you are going extra heavy, be careful. It's always best to have someone spotting you if you struggle to lift the weight back to the starting position.

SCORPION KICKS/GLUTE KICKBACKS

This is an easy and effective exercise that targets your glutes. Though not as effective as doing heavy squats, deadlifts, glute bridges etc., it is perfect for an exercise later on near the cool-down. This will feel like a 'top up' for your glutes and you should really feel it, especially after squatting or thrusting heavy weights!

Muscles worked: glutes, hamstrings, abdominals, hip flexors.

How: Kneel on the floor or an exercise mat and bend at the waist with your arms extended slightly in front of you in a kneeling push-up position, but with your arms spaced at shoulder width. Your head should be looking forward and the bend of the knees should create a 90-degree angle between the hamstrings and the calves. This will be your starting position.

As you exhale, lift up your right leg until the hamstrings are in line with your back while maintaining the 90-degree angle bend. Contract the glutes throughout this movement and hold the contraction at the top for a second. At the end of the movement the upper leg should be parallel to the floor while the calf should be perpendicular to it.

Go back to the initial position as you inhale and now repeat for the number of reps on the same leg. And then do the same on the other leg. Alternatively, you can alternate legs until all the recommended repetitions have been performed.

Progression: You can further engage your abdominals when bringing the knee down by bringing it in close to your tummy and past the sedentary leg. Or you can make it into a pulse by bringing the leg down by just 1-2 inches and then back up.

BIRD DOG

This is not an intense exercise but it is a great exercise to engage and activate your glutes after the warmup. It also engages your core.

Muscles worked: glutes, abdominals, shoulders.

How: Get on all fours with your arms straight under your shoulders. Keep knees hip width and tighten your abdominal muscles, keeping your spine and neck in a neutral position.

Slowly extend your left leg behind you while reaching your right arm forward. Keep your hips and shoulders square and make sure your lower back doesn't arch. Hold for 3-5 seconds. Return to the starting position then repeat the move on the opposite side.

SUPERMAN

This is known as a yoga style exercise, but it is a great way to strengthen your lower back and tone your ass. You are also working your abdominal muscles, which is always a bonus! (More ideas of how to use yoga to make your booty beautiful can be seen later in the book).

Muscles worked: abdominals, lower back, glutes, pectorals.

How: Lie on the floor, facing down with your body straight. Then fully extend your arms in front of you with your palms facing down. Simultaneously raise your arms, legs and chest off the floor. Hold the contraction for 5 seconds. As you raise your body parts, squeeze your lovely butt muscles hard and raise your legs off the ground further.

Lower your chest, arms and legs down and repeat for the desired number of repetitions.

Progression: Hold the contraction for 10 to 15 seconds and flutter your arms and legs up and down for the duration of the hold.

SIDE-LYING HIP ABDUCTION

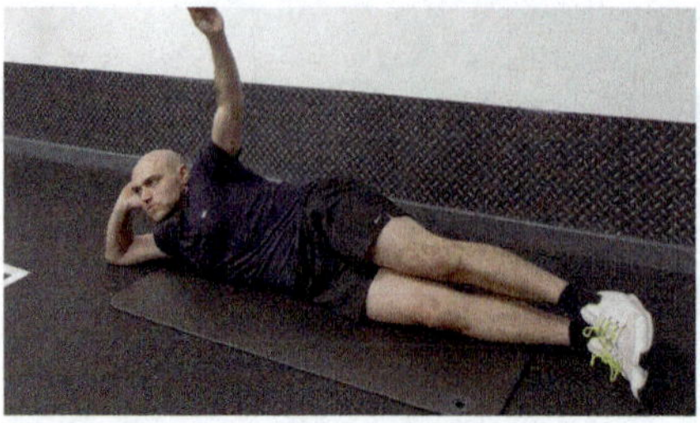

This is a very good exercise for working your upper glutes – the gluteus minimus and medius. It also improves flexibility in the inner thighs. After getting used to this, you can then master the more challenging side-lying hip raise.

Muscles worked: gluteus medius and minimus, abductors, adductors, abdominals (obliques to greater extent), hip flexors.

How: Lie on your side with your legs straight and your feet stacked one on top of the other in neutral position. Rest your head on your arm touching the floor or on the palm of your hand. Rest your top arm along your side or raise above your head.

Raise the upper leg until you feel a nice squeeze on the side of your ass. Keep your knees straight and your hips neutral. Don't let your hips roll forward or backwards.

Return to the starting position and repeat for the desired number of reps. Switch to the other side and execute the same movement for the desired number of reps.

Progression: This is uncomfortable but effective. As you raise your leg to the top of the movement, bring your leg down just a little bit so it's less than half way down. Raise your leg back up and repeat for as many times as you desire. Yes, I know it feels like your hip will fall off, but I swear it won't!

SIDE-LYING HIP RAISE

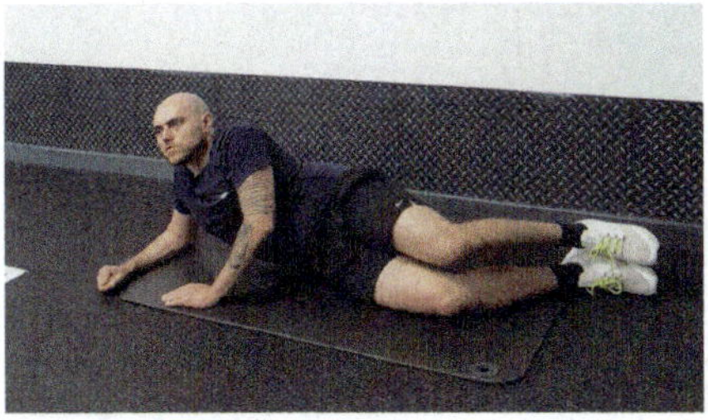

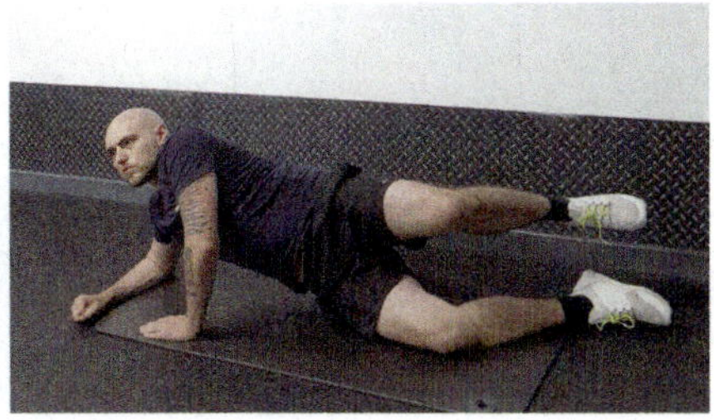

This looks very similar to the side-lying hip abduction. Although it looks similar, it is a lot more challenging on your hips, glutes and obliques. But this exercise is a good opportunity to gain size and strength on your upper glutes and also work your obliques, aka love handles!

Muscles worked: gluteus medius and minimus, abductors, adductors, abdominals (obliques to greater extent), hip flexors.

How: Start by lying on your right side, supporting your weight on your elbow with your arm positioned under your shoulder.

Bend your knees, placing your feet behind you with your left leg on top of your right leg. Keep your spine aligned by avoiding leaning forward or arching your back.

Now lift your top leg and move it upwards slightly towards the ceiling. Either straighten the top leg or have it bent.

Press up with your right hip but make sure your left leg is up during the movement.

Lower the hip back to the floor and repeat for the desired number of repetitions then switch onto the other side.

Progression: Hold for 5 seconds or longer at the top of the movement.

FIREARMS/FIRE HYDRANT

This exercise is easy and effective to perform. It really works your gluteus medius. This has a surprisingly good effect considering it is a bodyweight exercise. I nickname this exercise the 'dog pee', which isn't professional when I describe it, but you'll see what I mean.

Muscles worked: hip flexors, gluteus medius and minimus, abductors, adductors, abdominals (obliques to greater extent), hip flexors.

How: Begin on your hands and knees, with your knees positioned under your hips and your arms under your shoulders.

Keeping your knee bent, raise one leg as high as your hips and pause for a second. Return to the starting position and repeat for the desired number of reps on the same leg.

To make this more intense, one option is that when you raise your leg, hold and add a kick by moving your calf and foot outwards before returning to starting position.

Progression: After doing several standard fire hydrants, add a pulse by raising the leg up but only bringing it down by approximately 3 inches and raising it back up again. You'll feel this!

DOUBLE QUADRUPLED HIP ABDUCTION

This exercise is unique as it strengthens the upper glutes in a hips-flexed position, which is important for exercises such as squats and deadlifts. This may look like the fire hydrant but it has more of range of motion on the hips!

Muscles worked: gluteus medius and minimus, abductors, adductors, abdominals (obliques to greater extent).

How: Get on your hands and knees. Position your knees under your hips and arms under your shoulders. Start by shifting your weight to sink into your left side without twisting your upper body. As you sink, your right leg should hover off the floor.

Push both hips outward, lifting your right leg up to the side and you should feel your glutes work! Go back down into your left hip and repeat for the desired number of repetitions. Then repeat the same number of repetitions on the opposite side/leg.

Progression: Make a pulse out of this exercise, starting from the top of the movement by bringing your leg down just a little bit and then going back to the top of the movement and holding that position for 5 seconds.

STEP UPS

This is a deceptively effective lower body definer and strengthener (yep, gluteus maximus!). Start by using a box or bench that is 1-2 feet tall, or tall enough so your knee is in line with your hip. Remember, once you're comfortable, you can always go higher!

Muscles worked: glutes, quadriceps, hamstrings, calves, hip flexors.

How: Stand up straight, placing your hands on your hips. Place one foot on the elevated platform. Step on the platform by extending the hip and knee of the working leg. Use the heel to lift the rest of your body up and place the toes of the opposite leg on the platform. Exhale as you execute the force required to come up.

Step down with the opposite leg you went up with whilst inhaling. Return to starting position by stepping down with the leg still on the platform. Repeat by using the same leg for the recommended number of reps. Then do the same amount on the other leg.

Progression: There are MANY ways you can progress with this exercise:

As you step up with one leg, squeeze the glutes for a couple of seconds and step back down with the opposite leg.

Once you have gained confidence with this exercise, you can add weight to it by holding two dumbbells at your side. You can progress further by increasing the weight.

If you are ready for a challenge, you could use a barbell balanced across your shoulders and back. Execute using the same movement as you would with dumbbells. The barbell should be slightly below the neck.

Another way is to use a higher box/bench so that as you step up with one leg, your knee is higher than your hip. This gives your hip joint a lot more range of motion and is a fantastic booty builder. However, if you are adding weight, then I strongly recommend using dumbbells as opposed to a barbell for balance and safety purposes. By adding weight and using a high box/bench, you and your sexy glutes mean business!

BOX STEP-DOWN

This is very underrated and underused, despite being very similar to box step-ups. The higher the box you use, the bigger the range of motion you can do.

Muscles worked: glutes, quadriceps, hamstrings, calves, hip flexors.

How: Start by standing on a bench or box. Stand close to the edge so that you can step off it to the side with one foot.

Standing near the edge of the box with your other foot right on the side or hanging off, slowly hinge forward, sitting your butt back as you drop the foot on the side down toward the ground. Keeping your back flat, push your butt back as you bend your standing knee to drop your foot toward the ground.

If you can, lightly touch the toe of the foot to the ground, but make sure you do not drop it all the way down so that you can push off it. Sink as low as you can then drive right back up to standing. Make sure you are only driving through your standing heel and not using your foot on the ground.

Do not rock forwards as you come back up to standing. Really use your glutes and drive through your heel. Stand back up nice and tall and squeeze your glutes at the top.

Repeat for the recommended number of reps on the same leg. Repeat the same amount of reps on the opposite leg

Progression: Either use a higher box to give your hip joint a greater range of motion or add dumbbells at either side of you.

REVERSE LUNGE TO STEP-UP

I use this exercise often in my bootcamp classes. I think it is a challenging but effective exercise combo. The legs and glutes are going from working in the lunge to then doing the box step-up.

Muscles worked: glutes, hamstrings, quadriceps, hip flexors, abdominals.

How: Stand tall with your feet hip-distance apart then take a large step backward with one foot. Lower the back knee to a 90-degree angle so both knees are bent. After a very brief pause, bring the working knee back past the stationary leg and raise your foot onto the box. Use the heel to lift the rest of your body up and place the toes of the opposite leg on the platform. Exhale as you execute the force required to come up. Step down with the opposite leg you went up with. Return to starting position by stepping down with the leg still on the box. Repeat on the same or opposite leg for the recommended number of repetitions.

Progression: Either use a higher box to give your hip joint a greater range of motion or add dumbbells at either side of you, or a barbell across your back.

RUSSIAN KETTLEBELL SWING

This exercise may be very popular in circuit classes but the opportunity it gives to build the glutes is often left unsaid due to too many people not using enough weight. Try starting with a 4kg kettlebell to work out the technique and then use a kettlebell as heavy as you can whilst still executing the movement correctly. This also greatly impacts the hamstrings as well.

Muscles worked: glutes, hip flexors, hamstrings.

How: Stand behind the kettlebell, bend over at the hips and grab the handle of the kettlebell, stretching the hamstrings with your chest up. Hike the kettlebell backwards so it goes between and past the legs.

Then forcefully contract your hips and push the kettlebell forward with your glutes, keeping your arms straight and letting the momentum drive the load upwards, squeezing the glutes. Ensure that you are making your hips and glutes do the work and not your arms. Raise the kettlebell as high as you can as your hips push it upwards. Let gravity reverse the motion downwards.

As the kettlebell approaches your body when travelling downwards, use your arms to accelerate the motion onto your hips to engage the load onto the hamstrings and glutes. Keeping your chest tall, stretch the hamstrings with glutes, back, spine and neck in a neutral posture. Explode your hips forward and squeeze your glutes at the end. You will have built enough momentum to repeat the desired number of reps without stopping.

Progression: Increase the weight of the kettlebell.

CABLE EXERCISES

Whilst you are in the gym it is wise to make use of fixed equipment! If you've spent any time in a gym, there's a good chance you're familiar with the cable machine.

The cable machine is a large piece of gym equipment that has adjustable cable pulleys. The resistance of the cables allows you to perform numerous exercises in a variety of directions. Some machines have one or two cable stations, while others have multiple. Including cable exercises in your fitness routine is an excellent way to add variety to your workout.

ONE-LEGGED CABLE KICKBACK

This is not the most comfortable of exercises, but if performed correctly it will target your glute muscles.

Muscles worked: glutes, hamstrings, quadriceps, abdominals.

How: First, hook a leather ankle cuff to a low cable pulley and then attach the cuff to your ankle.

Face the weight stack from a distance of about two feet, grasping the steel frame for support.

While keeping your knees and hips bent slightly and your core tight, contract your glutes to slowly kick the working leg back in a semi-circular arc as high as it will comfortably go as you breathe out. When you are at full extension, squeeze your glutes for a second to achieve a peak contraction.

Slowly bring your working leg forward, resisting the pull of the cable until you reach the starting position.

Repeat for the recommended number of repetitions. And then switch legs and repeat the movement for the other side.

Progression: Increase the weight.

CABLE PULL THROUGH

This is a more comfortable cable exercise. If performed correctly, you can expect significant gains, although it is difficult to use heavy loads due to it affecting balance and stability.

Muscles worked: glutes, hamstrings, quadriceps, abdominals.

How: Begin by standing a few feet in front of a low pulley with a rope or handle attached. Face away from the machine, straddling the cable, with your feet set wide apart.

Start the movement by grabbing hold of the cable rope/bar with the cable between your legs, facing away from the cable column. Step out a couple of steps to put the cable on tension.

Whilst keeping the spine and neck in neutral position, sit back and bend at the hips. Then push forward with your hips by squeezing your glutes, making sure you reach full hip extension. Repeat this for the desired number of repetitions.

Alternatively, you can do a straight-legged pull through version. You execute it in the same way but keep your legs straight with only a very slight bend in the knees. This option targets the hamstrings more.

Progression: Increase the weight. With practice, you will soon be able to do so.

SIDE CABLE LEG RAISE

This cable exercise allows you to target your upper glutes and targets the hip abductors. The grounded leg works isometrically, whilst the free leg works dynamically.

Muscles worked: glutes, hamstrings, quadriceps, abdominals, hip flexors.

How: Stand in front of the cable pulley sideways on, with your feet hip-width apart. Have one leg next to the pulley and the other behind. Attach the ankle cuff to the ankle of the leg that you are going to work during the exercise (the one furthest from the machine).

Now step out and away from the stack with a wide stance and grasp the bar of the pulley system.

Stand on the foot that does not have the ankle cuff and allow the leg with the cuff to be pulled towards the low pulley. This will be your starting position.

Now perform the movement by moving the leg with the ankle cuff in front of the far leg by using the inner thighs to abduct the hip. Breathe out during this portion of the movement.

Slowly return to the starting position as you breathe in.

Repeat for the recommended amount of repetitions and then repeat the same movement with the opposite leg.

Progression: Increase the weight load on the cable.

PLYOMETRICS

Plyometric exercises are power exercises that use explosive amounts of energy. They lead to improvements in speed as well as strength. They have their own range of benefits compared to most exercises that rely on their rep ranges – strength, hypertrophy (which means muscle building, but more on that later) and endurance. Your muscles will become more powerful doing these exercises, which will greatly assist your strength and can only help your ass burn and grow!

SQUAT JUMPS

These are great for building power in the glutes, but there are also great for killing fat, killing calories and toning the core! This plyometrics exercise can also be done outdoors in a park or at home if you have a fair bit of space.

Muscles worked: glutes, hamstrings, quadriceps, abdominals.

How: Start with your arms by your side, feet shoulder-width apart, head up, and back straight.

Keeping your back straight and chest up, squat down as you inhale until your upper thighs are parallel, or lower, to the floor.

Now pressing mainly with the balls of your feet, jump straight up in the air as high as possible, using the thighs like springs. Exhale during this portion of the movement.

Land back on the ground with your feet in the same position as before you performed the jump squat.

Repeat this exercise for the duration of the given exercise time or number of recommended reps.

Progression: Make it into box squat jump. Squat down until your glutes merely touch the box and you explode up into the air.

BOX JUMPS

Another fantastic power exercise for power-loading the glutes and lower body, as well as being one of the top calorie burners, along with the jump squat. It might seem intimidating seeing people do this but if you start using a lower box, you will get the hang of this and work your way up using higher boxes and feel like a pro!

Muscles worked: glutes, hamstrings, quadriceps, abdominals.

How: Begin with a box of an appropriate height 1-2 feet in front of you. Stand with your feet shoulder-width apart. This will be your starting position.

Perform a short squat in preparation for jumping, swinging your arms behind you.

Rebound/jump out of this position, extending through the hips, knees, and ankles to jump as high as possible. Swing your arms forward and up.

Land on the box with the knees bent, absorbing the impact through the legs. You can jump from the box back to the ground, or preferably step down one leg at a time.

Repeat this exercise for the duration of the given exercise time or number of recommended reps.

TIP: If you are nervous about this exercise at first, ask to be shown by a professional or someone who regularly does these.

LUNGE JUMPS

So many people hate these, but love them or hate them, they have the same benefits as the jump squats and box jumps. They greatly improve balance and coordination. These exercises can also be done in a local park or indoors if there's enough space.

Muscles worked: glutes, hamstrings, quadriceps, abdominals, hip flexors.

How: Start with one leg forward and one leg back as if you were in the starting position of a bodyweight stationary lunge. Hold your arms crossed in front of you at chest height.

Bend your knees and sink downwards into a deep lunge. Lean forwards slightly and engage your core. This is to work your core muscles throughout the exercise.

As you sink your weight down fully but without the knee touching the floor, explosively launch your body upwards, fully extending your knees and hips. As you jump into the air, bring your feet together quickly and switch positions as your feet land back on the floor. Also, switch the position of your arms.

Maintain a balanced foot position; your forward knee should be above your forward foot and NOT further beyond it. Drop into a deep lunge position as you prepare for the next jump lunge.

Repeat this exercise for the duration of the given exercise time or number of recommended reps.

TIP: If it's a nice day and too nice to go the gym, why not run or walk to the park and do lots of sets or intervals of lunge jumps and jump squats and then walk back home?

RESISTANCE BANDS

Resistance bands are becoming increasingly popular. People include them in their workouts to assist with muscle growth, fat loss, strength, flexibility and other improvements in regards to fitness. But there are also the benefits in their convenience. Bands are handy for keeping at home as they take up very little space compared with free weights.

HOW RESISTANCE BANDS WORK

Every time you stretch a band, it gets heavier. For example, take a rubber band. When the band is unused, it is bouncy and flexible. The further you stretch it, however, the more tension you feel, and the more force you need to use to keep it taut. Resistance bands are just the same.

Resistance bands can drastically increase the intensity of exercises that would have been bodyweight, but not to the extent of free weights and/or resistance machines.

TIP: Buy a resistance band but only use it at home on days you cannot get to the gym. You pay your gym membership, make the most of the opportunity to progress from lighter to heavier weights. Get your money's worth from your membership!

Adding a resistance band adds extra tension and intensity to the majority of the exercises you will be doing a lot, such as deadlifts and goblet squats. However, here are some exercises that specifically benefit from the extra amount of hard work needed by adding a resistance band. Some of these exercises cannot be progressed with weights.

TIP: You could even make your own resistance programme for at home. This would be ideal if it was a hot sunny day and you wanted to spend the maximum amount of time in the garden. Or even on a beach to attract some hotties!!!

DEEP SQUAT

Adding a resistance band takes your typical squat to the next level as your glutes will have to work a lot harder to fight against the resistance from the band. As you will be squatting deeply, you will be squatting extra heavy even without any weight added!

How: Stand with feet shoulder-width apart, place the band around your thighs, just above your knees. Push your hips back and lower down to the ground until your thighs are parallel to the ground. Return to the starting position by squatting back up.

Progression: Try it as a goblet squat, holding a dumbbell vertically at chest height in front of you.

CURTSY LUNGE

Just like squats, resistance bands add intensity to lunges, including the beloved curtsy lunge!

Muscles worked: glutes, quadriceps, hamstrings, hip abductors and core.

How: Stand with your feet hip-width apart, with the band placed around your thighs. Step your left foot behind you and to the right, lowering your body until your right thigh is parallel to the floor. Return to standing. Perform for the desired amount of reps, then repeat on the opposite side.

Progression: Progress by holding a kettlebell in front of your chest or two dumbbells at your sides when you're ready to increase the intensity.

SINGLE-LEG DEADLIFT

The single-leg version of the deadlift really challenges your balance, which then strengthens your core strength as well as adding extra pressure on the leg executing the exercise. By adding a resistance band, you're adding even more pressure to the working leg.

How: Put a band under your right foot and hold it with your right hand. Split your stance by placing your right foot in front and left foot behind. Transfer your weight to your right leg. Ensure your back is straight and core engaged. Keeping your right knee slightly bent, slowly hinge forward at the hips. Lower your body so your hips go back and your shoulders go forward until your hand reaches your mid-calf. Stand back up to starting position. Perform the desired number of reps, then repeat on opposite side.

Progression: Add a kettlebell or dumbbell in the opposite hand.

SQUAT SIDE WALK

Adding a resistance band increases the resistance substantially in this exercise. Especially to the glutes, quadriceps and core!

How: Pull the resistance band around your legs, just above your knees or ankles, keeping your feet wide enough that you can feel the booty-burn! Lower your ass towards the ground into a squat position. Step sideways four or five times or until you are at the other end of the room, and repeat the other way. Repeat for the amount of side steps or wall touches you've set as a goal.

Progression: Make it extra, extra hard by placing a kettlebell in front of you.

STANDING GLUTE KICKBACKS

Adding a resistance band strengthens the glutes and hamstrings to a greater extent in this exercise.

How: Place the band around your ankles, standing with your feet hip-width apart and your core muscles engaged. Transfer your weight onto one leg, and with the opposite leg, slowly kick backwards as far as you can go as you squeeze your glutes at the top of the movement. Reverse the movement with control, and with your raised foot, gently tap the ground just behind your planted foot. Complete the desired amount of reps on one leg, then switch to the other.

GLUTE BRIDGES

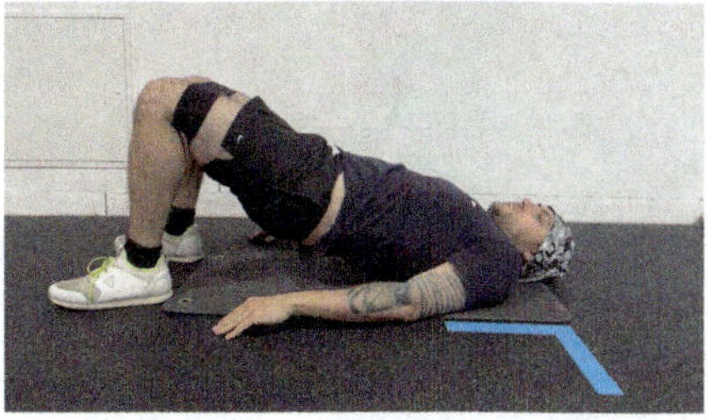

Another way to target the glutes and hamstrings even harder by using a resistance band.

How: Place the band above your knees. Lie on your back with your feet flat on the floor, hip-width apart. Engage your abs and squeeze your glutes as you press down through your heels to lift your hips and glutes off the floor, until your knees reach a 90-degree bend. Throughout the movement, push your knees out against the band to keep them in line with your shoulder width. Reverse back to starting position. Repeat for the desired number of reps.

Progression: Make it harder by lifting one foot off the ground an inch and pushing solely with the opposite leg. Alternate reps.

SIDE-LYING LEG LIFTS

This is already a killer, but by adding a band you are strengthening the hip-abductor muscles even more.

How: Place the band above your knees. Lie on your side with your legs straight and stacked one on top of the other. Lift your upper leg towards the ceiling as high as you can without lifting your hip off the ground, then slowly lower it for one repetition. Keep your upper leg in line with your bottom leg throughout the movement. Repeat for the desired number of repetitions.

SINGLE-LEG SIT TO SQUAT

This is an epic exercise for strengthening the quads and gluteus maximus, whilst improving stability.

How: Place the band above your knees. Sit on the edge of a bench or chair, ideally one at a height where your knees are bent to 90 degrees when sitting. Move your upper-body forward slightly so that your chest is in front of your hips. Then lift one foot off the floor by an inch or so, and with the opposite foot firmly planted on the ground, stand up on that one leg until it is fully extended. Keep a consistent hip-width space between your knees throughout the movement.

Return to a seated position for one repetition and repeat for the desired number of reps.

Progression: You can use a lower bench or chair. Alternatively, hold a kettlebell in front of your chest to add weight and workload. You can progress even further by increasing the intensity using a lower chair and by adding weight.

CLAMSHELLS

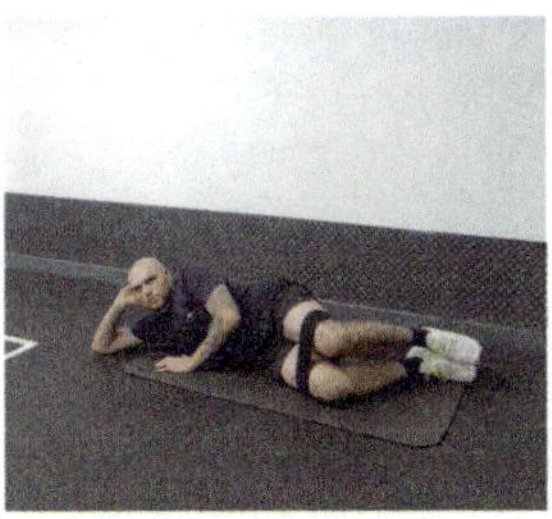

If you are a big fan of working your abs and bootiez, this is right up your street! The added resistance band strengthens the gluteus medius and obliques even further!

How: Place the band above your knees and lie on your side, with your knees bent to 90 degrees. Prop your head up on your hand or support yourself with your lower arm. Engage your core, keeping your feet pressed together, and drive your top knee toward the ceiling as far as you can whilst keeping the form. Slowly bring it down to starting position. Repeat for the desired number of reps.

ABDOMINAL/CORE EXERCISES

I have added some Abdominal (abs) and Core-strength exercises to the 38-session programme for many reasons. Core-strength exercises work the muscles in many important muscle groups, such as the pelvis, lower back, hips and the abs of course! This then leads to better balance, stability and core strength.

This makes it easier to do most physical activities or chores. A very good example would be if you were to stand on a chair to reach something you had hidden on top of the cupboard. Your improved abdominal muscles would make this easier by having stronger abs and better balance.

Getting strong core muscles is important for so many athletes, such as runners, weightlifters or even basketball players. This is because weak core muscles can lead to earlier fatigue, reduced endurance, and increased chance of injury.

Weak core muscles can leave you with an increased risk of poor posture. Which could then lead to lower back pain and injuries on the muscles and joints. A stronger core has been known to improve lower back pain – something too many of us suffer from!

FACT: Your CORE and your ABS are not the same.

So what is the difference between your CORE and your ABDOMINALS? It is easy to get them confused. Many people believe they are the same thing. In fact, not that long ago, I thought the core meant the abdominal muscles.

Abs refer to your abdominal muscles. These include the rectus abdominis, the top layer of abdominal muscles that create a six-pack look when you exercise hard and eat sensibly. There's the transverse abdominis, which are the super-deep muscles that wrap around the stomach. These are a lot less visible than the rectus abdominis. And there are the internal and external obliques, which are the muscles on the side of your abs.

Your core, on the other hand, is made up of so much more. It includes the muscles in your pelvis, lower back, hips and abdominals.

Having a generous Bum:Tum ratio (big glutes, small belly) is a very desirable trend for the guyz and galz. The opposite is a big belly, small booty – LITERALLY A HORROR MOVIE FOR ME! If you are a lady in your bikini or a guy in your Speedos, you want to look good front AND back! A nice set of abs and a big sexy booty is a nice treat to the eye on the beach!

Although you will be working your abdominals in many important exercises in the 38-session programme, such as in the squats and deadlifts, I have added some abdominal exercises as a 'top up' to your workout. I hope this helps you achieve a body you are proud to have!

There are SO many core strength/abdominal exercises, but I have included a small but sweet amount of them to ensure that the upper abs, lower abs and obliques (side abs) are all covered.

PLANK EXERCISES

Almost everyone has heard of this excellent but tough abdominal and core strength exercise. Some people love it as you can create a plank challenge when working out with your friends. Some people hate it as it can be boring by being in a holding position, which can make it feel longer than it actually is.

FOREARM PLANK

Muscles worked: abdominals (rectus and transverse abdominus), obliques, quadriceps, lower back, hip flexors, glutes.

How: Start in a press-up position (also known as a push-up plank). Bend your elbows until your forearms are on the floor beneath your shoulders so your body is in a straight line from your feet to your head. Keep your abs tight and look at the space between your hands to ensure a neutral spine position. Hold the position for the desired amount of time.

TIP: Many mistakes are made in this exercise. Try to avoid these mistakes to get the most out of the exercise and avoid discomfort, strain or injury.

By following this guidance you shouldn't have any problems.

Avoid arching your back: If your back is arched in the plank, you are not engaging your abdominals sufficiently and you are shifting more of the weight to your arms. This can also be painful for your back.

Avoid tilting your head up: keep your neck in line with your body as opposed to being tilted up. This can strain the neck.

Avoid dropping your hips close to the floor as this puts your lower back into an uncomfortable position. Keeping your core in tight towards your spine can help avoid dropping the hips. If you are struggling to do this, it may be a sign of fatigue. Maybe make it easier by having your feet at a wider stance.

Progression: Increase the amount of time spent on this exercise, possibly even hold the position for as long as you can.

There are SO many variations to this exercise to make it harder. You could bring one knee in close to your elbow on the same side and then repeat on the opposite side. This engages your obliques more and puts more pressure on the core by making it heavier by having one leg off the floor.

Another way to engage your obliques more is to twist/rotate one hip down close to the floor and hold whilst in plank position – burner!

PLANK TO FOREARM PLANK

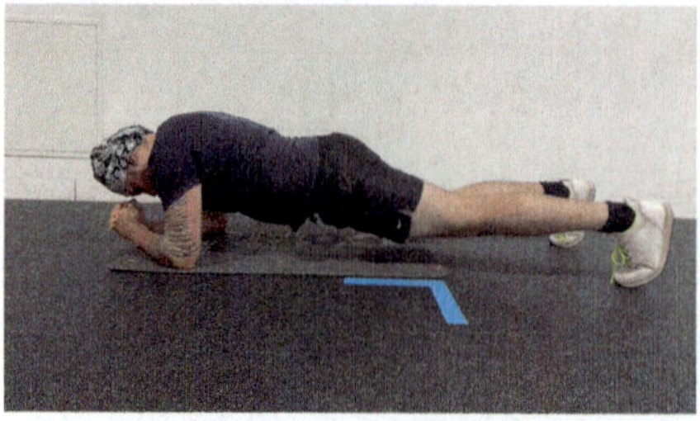

Being in a plank position for a certain period of time can be extremely boring and you can easily get distracted, which is off-putting when you are trying to work hard. This plank alternative exercise adds intensity as although you are in plank position, you are working your core hard throughout as you are using it from push-up plank to forearm plank. This exercise keeps your mind busy and distracts it from the toughness on your abs during the exercise – though once you've finished, you WILL feel it!

Muscles worked: abdominals (rectus and transverse abdominis), obliques, quadriceps, lower back, glutes.

How: To perform the move, start in a forearm plank position on the ground (on your elbows, forearms and toes). Keep a straight spine and squeeze your beautiful glutes.

Lift yourself up one arm at a time and straighten your elbows until you are in a push-up plank position. Maintain your spine's alignment and keep squeezing your glutes. Lower your elbows, one arm at a time, to the ground into forearm plank position.

Progression: One way to make this exercise even more interesting is to add a few extras when you are in both push-up and forearm plank position – but I warn you that it is a sweaty challenge!

When in push-up plank, bring one knee to the elbow on the opposite side (e.g left knee to right elbow) and repeat with the other knee.

When in forearm plank, bring one knee to your elbow on the same side (e.g. left knee to left elbow) and repeat with the other knee.

SIDE PLANK

This popular oblique-focused exercise not only works the oblique muscles, it also strengthens your core muscles without putting excess stress on the lower back. It is a great way for boosting your balance as keeping in balance is part of the challenge!

Muscles worked: obliques, abdominals (rectus and transverse abdominis).

TIP: Use a mat or other soft surface whilst performing this exercise. This will help reduce the amount of stress on your arms and feet.

How: Lie on your side with your forearm flat on the floor, bottom elbow lined up directly under your shoulder and both legs extended out in a long line. Your feet can either be staggered for more stability or stacked to make it more challenging. Whilst engaging your core, lift your hips off the floor forming a straight line from your head to your feet. You can either place your top hand by your hip, or to make it harder, reach up to the ceiling. Hold for the desired amount of time then repeat on the opposite side.

Progression: Once you are able to execute this exercise by reaching up to the ceiling, try mastering this side plank rotation also known as under the bridge.

SIDE PLANK ROTATION

How: Whilst you are in side plank position with your arm straight above you, lower your arm and rotate your core as you bring your top arm through the space that is underneath your body and above the floor. Once your shoulders are almost parallel to the floor, return to starting position. You WILL feel this!

CRUNCHES

There are many types on crunches, and we will start with the standard variation. They target the rectus abdominis, the six-pack muscle that runs along the front of the torso.

CRUNCH

Muscles worked: abdominals (rectus and transverse abdominis).

How: Lie on your back. Plant your feet on the floor at hip-width apart. Bend your knees and place your arms across your chest. Contract your abdominal muscles and inhale. Exhale and lift your upper body, keeping your head and neck relaxed. Return to the starting position and complete for the desired amount of reps or time spent on the set.

TIP: Use your core to raise your upper body. If the movement comes from your head or neck, you'll increase the risk for injury, so avoid pulling on the neck.

Progression: Add some weight by holding a weight plate or light medicine ball at your chest.

REVERSE CRUNCHES

This really targets the rectus abdominis (also known as the six-pack muscles) but more so the lower abs.

FACT: Lower abdominal definition is hard to achieve as it is where the body stores a LOT of excess fat.

Unfortunately, the glamorous thought of having well-defined, eye-catching abs really does clash with poor lifestyle habits, especially eating and drinking things we really enjoy such as beer, wine, pizza and fries.

It has been known, however, that it is possible to achieve great abs whilst still having the odd beer and pizza night here and there. But this is providing you up your game with exercise (such as the 38-session programme!) and working your core.

Muscles worked: abdominals (rectus and transverse abdominis), especially the lower abs, obliques (to a lesser extent).

How: Lie on your back, arms by your side with palms facing down to help create the balance needed for the lift. Bend your legs at the knee and raise your legs so your knees are positioned directly above your hips, and your lower legs are parallel to the floor.

Pressing into your palms and engaging your core, lift your hips off the floor by bringing your knees in toward your chest until your hips come off the floor. Hold the crunch at the top of the movement, then begin to lower your hips and slowly return to the starting position so your knees return parallel to your hips. Repeat for the desired number of repetitions.

Progression: Engage your obliques. As your knees come in and hips come off the floor, twist your knees to one side whilst engaging your oblique muscles. Return to the starting position and repeat on the other side. On this variation, you are working your rectus abdominis and obliques hard.

BICYCLE CRUNCHES

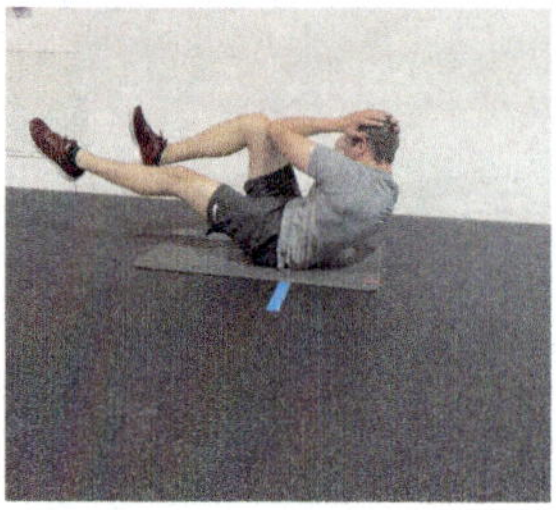

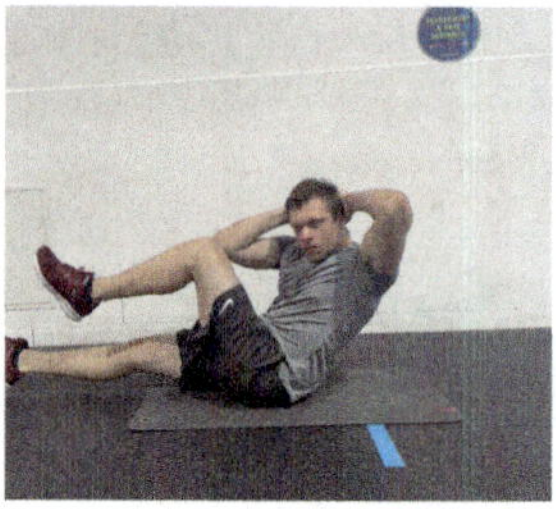

This is a core exercise which is a great alternative to crunches and I find it rather enjoyable but my abs don't!

Muscles worked: abdominals (rectus and transverse abdominis), obliques.

How: Lie flat on the floor with your lower back pressed into your mat. Place your hands behind your head with your fingers interlaced, keeping your elbows wide. Raise your legs up to a table top position (ankles in line with knees). Engage your abdominals and lift your head, so your shoulder blades are hovering off the ground. Straighten one leg long (for example, the left side) while turning the upper body to the opposite side (right) of the straightened leg.

Bring your left elbow towards your right knee. Avoid pulling on your neck but use your abdominals to lift. Twist at the ribs and lead with your shoulder rather than your elbow. Switch and repeat on the other side. Repeat for the desired amount of reps or time spent on this set.

Progression: Rather than switch sides, do a set all on one side. Then on the next set, do it on the opposite side. For example, 1st set is left elbow to right knee, the 2nd is right elbow to left knee. Most people I teach find this most challenging on the abs.

V-SIT CRUNCHES

This intense ab exercise builds core strength by working multiple areas of your core at the same time, while also challenging your balance. It is a LOT harder than it looks but surprisingly, I find this exercise rather more-ish!

Muscles worked: abdominals (rectus and transverse abdominis), obliques, hip flexors, lower back.

How: Lie flat on the ground with your arms by your sides. Raise your legs as high as you can, keeping them straight and together, and lift your torso up towards your thighs so you form a V-shape. Reach your arms straight forward or reach up toward your shins and hold this position for several seconds. Ensure you contract your abdominal muscles and keep a good posture. Avoid rounding your shoulders forward.

Return to your starting position slowly while continuing to keep your abs engaged and tight, but before you reach the floor, stop and hold the position for a few seconds. Repeat for the desired amount of reps or time spent on this set.

Progression: One way to make this exercise even more of a killer is to never lay back down into the starting position. Once you have paused at the movement for a few seconds whilst your back and legs are just off the floor, return so you are back into the V-shape.

TIP: Avoid rounding the back and shoulders whilst you are in V-sit position. Bending your back forward takes the focus off the core and puts a strain on the lower back, leaving less control work for your abs, making the exercise less effective and may lead to injury. The correct way is to maintain a straight line from your lower back up through your back, neck, and head. Your body should stay straight from starting position and throughout the movement.

LEG RAISES

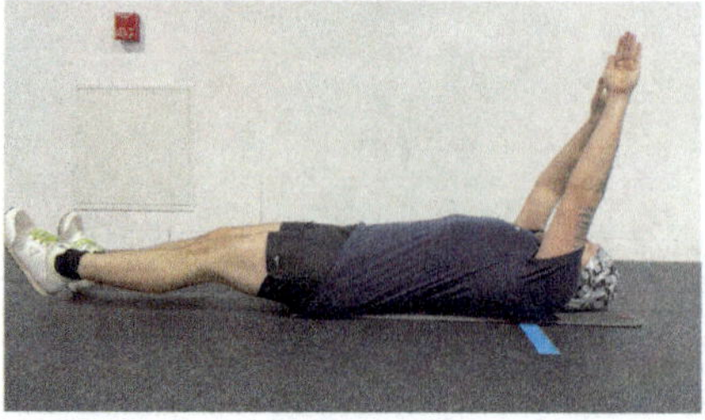 

A very popular abdominal exercise. Like the reverse crunches, they target your stubborn lower abdominal muscles and your lower back and therefore increase your core strength and the flexibility of your hips and lower back. This exercise is a pretty simple but effective exercise because it so often feels easy-peasy on the first rep but savage whilst you on your last rep or your thinking 'BITCH, I'M DONE!'

Muscles worked: abdominals (rectus and transverse abdominis), obliques, hip flexors, lower back.

How: Lie on your back, legs straight and together. Whilst keeping your legs straight, lift them all the way up to the ceiling until your butt comes off the floor. Slowly lower your legs back down until they're just above the floor. Hold for a short moment. Raise your legs back up and repeat for the desired amount of reps or time spent on this set.

Progression: Hold a kettlebell or weight-plate above your chest with your arms extended. The weight will add intensity to the exercise and your core, especially your abs.

FACT: If your legs are fatigued from working your ass hard at the gym or if you've been for a long run or been to a bootcamp, it will be very difficult to keep your legs straight.

An alternative is to grip a medicine ball between your feet whilst doing the exercise.

It is more difficult to keep your legs straight when they are tired because your legs are worked-up and your body is automatically making it easier by bending at the knees. When your lower body is fatigued, your legs have far less ability to straighten during a tough abdominal exercise. If you feel this is the scenario when you are in the 38-session programme, opt for the single leg variation. Keeping one leg towards the ceiling will help stabilise your body as you raise the other leg so you can focus on perfecting your form.

TIP: One common mistake is allowing the lower back to arch too much. This strains your back and may cause injury, pain and discomfort. It also makes the move much less effective, especially on your abdominals. If you are not keeping your back muscles and abdominals contracted, you are only working your hip flexors.

BOTTOMS UP

Probably my favourite abdominal exercise! This lying leg lift exercise is a popular bodyweight exercise targeting the muscles of the abs, especially for your lower abdominal region. While you are focusing on reaching the ceiling with your feet and then bringing them back down and out away from your body, your abs are working very hard.

This exercise is a great progression to continue burning your lower abs once reverse crunches become too easy for you.

Muscles worked: abdominals (rectus and transverse abdominis), especially the lower abs, obliques (lesser extent), gluteus maximus.

How: Lie flat on the ground with your legs straight. Raise your feet off the floor slightly and bring your knees up to your chest and extend your legs above you, then lift your glutes from the floor to push your legs as high as you can. Smoothly return, under control, to the start position without letting your legs touch the ground until you have completed the desired amount of reps or time spent on this set.

Progression: On the last repetition, once your knees come back down into your chest, bring your legs out slowly and when your legs are straightened, pause for a second before allowing your feet to touch the floor. You will realise this is a progression when you feel it – trust me!!!!

MASON TWIST

Also known as Russian twist. You may have seen many people in the gym performing these exercises. They primarily target your obliques, but also substantially engage your centre abdominal muscles as you are in a V-sit position throughout the exercise. They also work your lower back.

Muscles worked: abdominals (rectus and transverse abdominis), obliques, lower back, latissimus dorsi, hip flexors.

How: Start by sitting on the floor with your knees bent and feet flat on the ground. Lean back so your upper body is at a 45-degree angle to the floor, or until you feel your abdominal muscles engaged. Keep your back straight at this angle throughout the exercise, as it will be tempting to hunch your shoulders forward and you may arch your back. Link/clasp your hands together in front of your chest, then brace your core and raise your legs up off the ground. Use your abdominals to twist your body over to one side, then do the same in the other direction. Count that as one rep and repeat for the desired amount of reps or time spent on the set.

Progression: Once you master this exercise with your feet grounded, raise your feet slightly off the ground. Also, straighten your legs so you are in a banana shape.

Adding a weight plate or medicine ball by holding them in your palms by your chest is a popular way to increase the intensity. You can progress further by increasing the weight.

BURPEES

This exercise is dreaded by many for a reason! It is a versatile abdominal exercise as it targets your abs, but if done intensely, it can be a big fat burner! You are using your abs when you are briefly going from squat position to push-up plank position, yet a high amount of energy is required and therefore a lot of calories are being burned. It also works a lot more muscles of the body than you would think as you are engaging a lot of your upper body and your legs – including your fantastic booty!

Muscles worked: rectus abdominis, glutes maximus, deltoids (shoulders), quadriceps, hamstrings, calves.

How: Start by standing with your feet shoulder-width apart and your arms by your sides. Lower into a squat position and place your hands on the floor. Kick or step your legs back into a plank position. Kick back to make it more intense. Jump or step your legs forward to return to a squat position. As you return to the standing position, jump upwards. Repeat for the desired amount of reps or time spent on this set.

Progression: Increase the speed of the movement, or as your legs come out so you are in push-up plank position, come down into a forearm plank and give your abs more work. Then come back up into push-up plank position to complete the repetition.

FROGGERS

Like burpees, this is another terrific exercise that helps strengthen the core, tone the glutes and burn calories due to the cardiovascular performance required.

Muscles worked: rectus abdominis, gluteus maximus, lower back, deltoids (at the front), hamstrings, quadriceps, calves.

How: Begin in push-up plank position with your body in a straight line and your legs and arms shoulder-width apart. Your hands should be shoulder-width apart directly beneath your shoulders. Jump forward into a wide squat position so your knees and feet should land outside of your elbows like a frog. Jump back into the plank position and repeat for the desired amount of reps or time spent on the set.

Progression: Perform this at a faster pace or add a jump (like when you do burpees) when your legs are at the side of your arms.

MOUNTAIN CLIMBERS

This is an intense ab exercise and you can execute this exercise fast or slow. You work your abs whilst you are in push-up plank position, yet the hard part is when you really engage your abs by bringing your knees close to your upper body.

Muscles worked: rectus abdominis, obliques (lesser extent).

How: Start in a press-up plank position with your hands shoulder-width apart directly beneath your shoulders. Pull one knee towards your chest without letting it touch the floor then return to the start position and do the same with the opposite leg. Repeat for the desired amount of reps or time spent on this set.

TIP: If you have lots of energy then do this at a fast pace but ensure you bring your knees in close to your chest. Bringing your knees in close is a priority. If you are lacking the energy, then maybe execute the exercise at a slower pace.

Progression: Try to perform this exercise at its best by doing it at a fast pace and by bringing your feet as close to your chest as possible.

FLEXIBILITY/STRETCHING AND MOBILITY

This is too often ignored by guys and girls. There are pre-workout stretches and post-workout stretches as well as static and dynamic stretches. You must make time to fit these in during any exercise regime.

Flexibility is extremely important for working out and recovery after working out. Stretching keeps the muscles flexible, strong and healthy! We want healthy glutes, right?

Without stretching, the muscles become tight. Then on training days, during activity, they become unable to extend all the way. This increases the risk of joint pain, strains and muscle damage. If you have a sedentary job, such as in an office, you are at even more risk of injury. Sitting in a chair results in tight hamstrings at the back of the thigh and stretching is then badly needed, whether you work out or not. If your muscles are tight, weak and/or injured, they may not be strong enough to support the joints and therefore you risk injury.

DIFFERENCE BETWEEN STATIC AND DYNAMIC STRETCHES

Dynamic stretching is a strategy used to improve mobility while moving through a range of motion. Static stretching, on the other hand, is performed by holding a stretch without movement for 10 seconds or more.

PRE-WORKOUT STRETCHES

TIP: To put it simply, dynamic stretching is performed with/during movement whereas static stretching is performed without.

These are exercises you do before each workout on your 38-session programme. They will keep the lower body and back relaxed, strong and flexible.

CALF STEP-BACKS – DYNAMIC

How: Stand straight with your hands by your side. Start on one leg by stepping back by approximately 2 feet. As you step back, step onto your forefoot and then onto your ankle. You should feel a nice stretch on your calf muscle. Repeat on the opposite side.

FORWARD TO BACKWARD LEG SWINGS – DYNAMIC

How: Support the body by holding one arm or palm out against a wall at shoulder height. Start with both feet directly under the hips and swing the outside leg forward and backwards. Continue doing these swings as you gradually increase the range of motion until the leg swings as far as it can go.

Repeat by turning so that your opposite leg is now on the outside and execute the same movement. Make sure your back is straight at all times, with the body stable and balanced.

SIDE TO SIDE LEG SWING – DYNAMIC

How: Start by facing a wall or something else for support. Brace the body with both arms outstretched or have your palms on the wall at shoulder height.

Swing one leg out to the side of the body, extending to a height that is comfortable. Swing the leg back crossing in front of the body. Increase the range of motion gradually until reaching the maximum comfortable height.

Make sure the back is straight at all times, with the body stable and balanced.

TRUNK ROTATION WITH MEDICINE BALL – DYNAMIC

TIP: This can also be done without a medicine ball with your palms placed in front of your chest as though in prayer.

How: Start by holding a light medicine ball and your feet hip-width apart. Hold the ball close to the body at chest height, with your hands at the middle of your body and your elbows bent. Engage your core muscles to stiffen your torso.

Whilst exhaling, slowly rotate your torso in one direction, keeping your upper arms at your sides and your hands at chest height. As you perform this movement, your head, chest and torso should all move together. Avoid arching your back. As you get to the end position, pause briefly and rotate back to starting position and then rotate in the opposite direction.

ARM CIRCLES – DYNAMIC

You will be working your arms a lot in exercises such as deadlifts, front squats, goblet squats and more, so it is important that you warm them up before starting.

How: Stand with your feet shoulder-width apart and extend your arms parallel to the floor.

Circle your arms forward using small controlled motions, gradually making the circles bigger until you feel a stretch in your triceps.

Reverse the direction of the circles after approximately 10 seconds.

MOBILITY EXERCISES

Mobility exercises are joint-related exercises. The exercises here are to improve movement in the joints you will be using on the 38-session programme. You will also feel a nice stretch.

SQUAT TO STAND – DYNAMIC

How: Stand with your feet hip-width apart. Whilst keeping your back flat (no arching of the back), lean down and grab your toes. This will be your starting position. Once you have grabbed your toes, squat down as low as you can go.

Squat back up and try to keep hold of the toes. Your legs should be almost straight and your hips and ass back and your hips backwards and upwards. Pause for 2 seconds as you feel a deep stretch in the hamstrings.

LUNGE WITH SPINAL ROTATION/TWIST – DYNAMIC

How: With your right leg, step forward and bend your left knee right down into a deep lunge. Your right knee should be aligned over your ankle.

Rotate forward and inward, bringing your left hand to your right toe. Place your right hand on your hip but don't put a lot of pressure on it. Rotate upwards and outwards to the right while opening the chest.

KNEE HUG WALK – DYNAMIC

How: Stand with your feet shoulder-width apart and raise one knee upwards and hug it into your chest, then step your knee down in front of you as you repeat on the opposite leg.

Continue by alternating legs.

POST-WORKOUT STRETCHES

These are exercises you perform after a workout. They should only take a total of 5 minutes to complete.

HAMSTRINGS – STATIC

How: Lie on your back and raise your right leg. Hold your right leg by placing your hands on your calf muscle. If you cannot grab your calf, then place your hands below your knee. Avoid placing your hands in the knee socket.

Whilst keeping your left leg straight with your foot on the floor, pull your right leg towards you until you feel a mild discomfort (no pain!). Hold for 10-15 seconds. Release and repeat with the opposite leg.

GLUTE STRETCH – STATIC

How: Lie on your back and bring your knees up to your chest. Cross your right leg over your left thigh. Grab the back of your left thigh with both hands. Avoid placing your hands in the knee socket.

Pull your left leg towards your chest and hold for 10-15 seconds. Repeat with the opposite leg.

INNER THIGH STRETCH – STATIC

How: Sit on the floor with your back straight and your legs bent. Put the soles of your feet together. Grab hold of your ankles and have your elbows resting on your inner thigh. Press your elbows into your thighs until you feel a mild discomfort (no pain) and hold for 10-15 seconds.

QUADRICEPS – STATIC

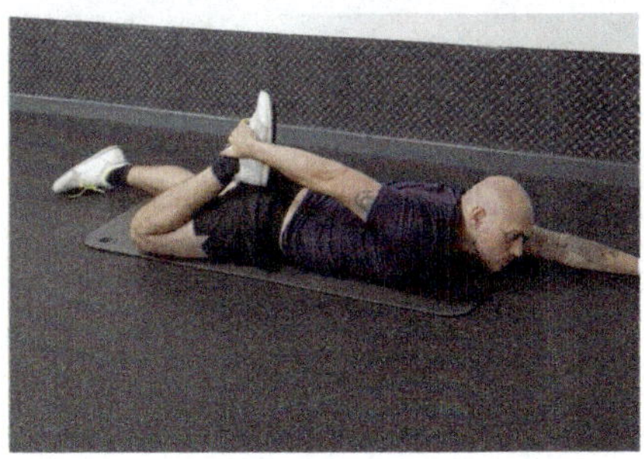

How: Lie on your front. Bring your right foot towards your right ass cheek and grab the top of your right foot. Pull your heel towards your right buttock to stretch out the quadricep. Hold for 10-15 seconds. Repeat on the opposite side.

Alternatively, you can do this lying on your side.

CALF STRETCH – STATIC

How: Face a wall and stand approximately 12 inches away from it. Extend your left leg behind you and keep both feet flat on the floor and your rear knee straight. Lean towards the wall until you feel tension in the calf muscle of the extended leg. Hold for 10-15 seconds. Repeat on the opposite leg.

COBRA POSE – STATIC

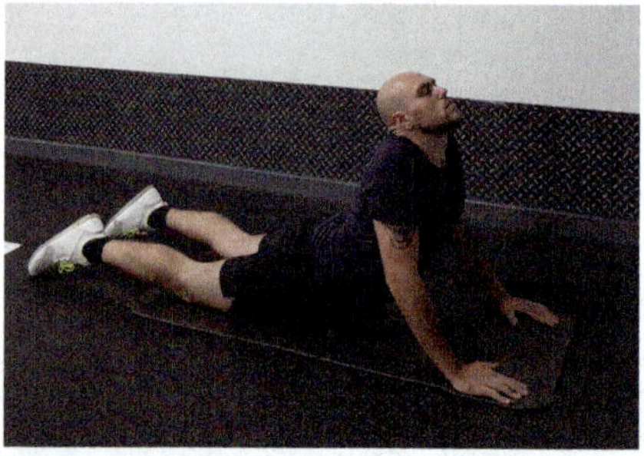

How: Lie face down, placing your palms next to your chest on either side, so you are at the bottom of a push up position.

With your hips staying in contact with the ground, point your feet downward and very slowly push your torso up as far as you feel comfortable. You should feel the stretch in the abdominals.

CHILD'S POSE – STATIC

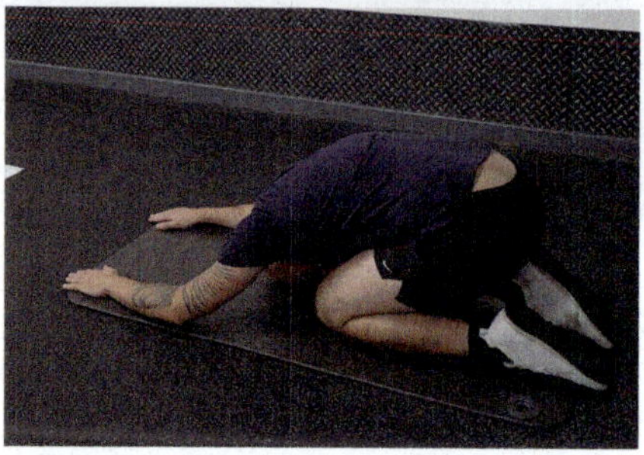

How: Begin on your hands and knees, then walk your hands in front of you. Lower your glutes down to sit on your heels, letting your arms drag along the floor as you sit back to stretch your spine.

Rest your forehead to the floor. You should feel a stretch in the lower back muscles. If you are unable to bend far enough for your forehead to reach the floor, don't worry.

TECHNICALITIES AND POLITICS OF TRAINING

Before you get in action and hit the 38-session programme, I have some useful information that will help you progress whilst you are in the training programme. Half-way through the book you will understand the importance of these sections.

REPETITION RANGES

Repetition (rep) ranges are split into 3 categories:
Strength, Hypertrophy and Endurance.

Strength	1-6 reps – high weight/low reps
Hypertrophy	6-12 reps – moderate weight/moderate reps
Endurance	12-20 reps – low weight/high reps

As we want to gain size and definition to our booty, hypertrophy is going to be our primary training method. Strength and endurance also have their own benefits and you will see some gains. During the training programme, you will mainly vary between 5-15 reps.

STRENGTH

People who do the strength rep ranges are usually wanting to get stronger – obviously! This method is also considered the most effective method for fat loss in comparison to hypertrophy and endurance. People who do strength training generally have a leaner physique. Other benefits to strength training are:

- Increased motor unit synchronisation and involvement.
- A more efficient and effective nervous system in the body. The nervous system helps all the parts of the body to communicate with each other. It also reacts to changes both outside and inside the body.
- Increased muscle force which then enables the muscles to perform more high-intense exercises
- Increased anaerobic performance – Creatine Phosphate system

The advised rest between sets for strength training is 2-4 minutes.

HYPERTROPHY

You will mainly be doing hypertrophy in the training programme as this is the rep range which will give you size and/or definition, depending on your diet. Bodybuilders normally use this type of training as their muscles will grow faster as they recover after training. You will still get a lot stronger training hypertrophy, especially if you do lots of rep ranges between 6-8 reps. This is commonly known as muscular strength training, where size and strength mix.

Hypertrophy training can also mix with endurance if rep ranges are close to 12. In a nutshell, the main benefits for training hypertrophy are:

- Increase in muscle mass
- Build in HGH (growth hormone)
- Increase in testosterone in men
- Increased anaerobic performance – Lactic Acid system.

The advised rest between sets for hypertrophy training is 1-2 minutes.

ENDURANCE

This rep range is about stamina. People doing endurance training might be training for a marathon or any other sport that involves a lot of stamina, such as a long bike ride. Or they may not want to build a great amount of muscle but still gain definition. An endurance workout normally lasts about 60-90 minutes ideally. Endurance training is great for toning and you can still gain a reasonable amount of muscle mass if the rep ranges are between 12-15 reps. This is also known as Muscular Endurance Training. I have given you some 15-20 reps on the programs, but only as warm-up sets.

Other valuable benefits of endurance training are:

- Increased stamina
- Muscle tone
- Increase in stroke volume
- Increased number of capillaries
- Increased metabolic response and rate
- Increased movement skill.

The advised rest between sets for endurance training is 30 seconds – 1 minute.

REST BETWEEN SETS

I advise to rest for 60-90 seconds between sets so you can do the required number of sets within an hour. If you are not doing a superset (when you pair exercises up), please limit the rest period to 60 seconds. If you had a 2-minute break after every set, it would use up 10 minutes of your sessions, which could be put to much better use, such as extra sets!

THINK
GO BIG OR GO HOME!

HOW LONG SHOULD A WORKOUT BE?

Please keep it as close to an hour as possible. Going too much over an hour will affect your recovery and cause you to overtrain and may increase stress levels, which in turn affect gains to size and strength.

TYPES OF TRAINING SETS

STRAIGHT SETS

Straight sets require you to perform a number of sets using the same weight and same number of repetitions. An example of this would be 4 sets of 10 reps on the barbell squat with the same amount of weight on each set.

PYRAMID SETS

This is where you alter the weight used and repetitions performed as you progress through the workout. For example, 1st set is 12 reps of 30 pounds, 2nd set is 10 reps of 35 pounds and 3rd set is 8 reps of 40 pounds. You could then go back down to 10 reps of 35 pounds and then 12 reps of 30 pounds. However, you may not be able to do the same amount of reps as you go back down. On the flipside, you may be able to do more!

Pyramid sets allow you to warm up gradually as you increase the intensity of your workout. It is also a good way to increase strength, hypertrophy and endurance. For example, if your first set was 15 reps of 25 pounds, then your second set would be 10 reps of 35 pounds and third set would be 5 reps of 45 pounds. You will be using pyramid sets on many occasions on your 38-session programme.

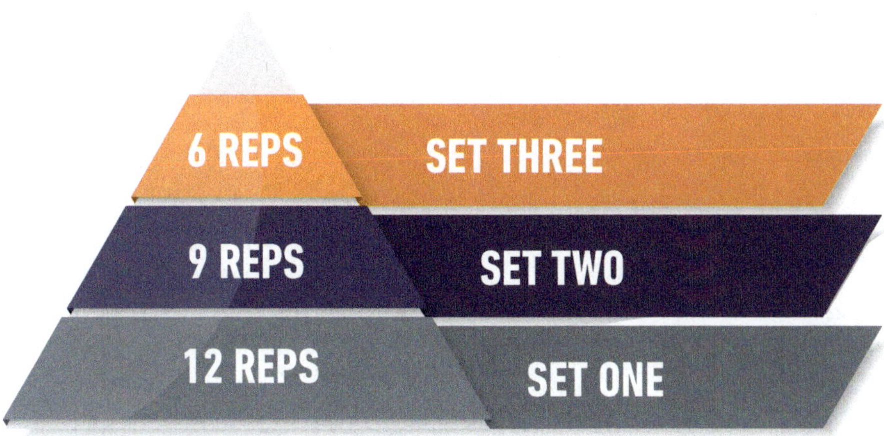

SUPERSETS

Also known as super-setting, this is where you pair exercises up. In these instances, you do not rest between pairings but only on completion of the second exercise of the superset. Supersets are a good way of increasing the intensity of the workout by reducing the amount of time you rest. You will also be doing lots of super-setting in your 38-session programme!

THERE ARE MANY TYPES OF SUPER-SETTING

Antagonist supersets:	When you pair exercises that work the same or similar muscles. An example would be sumo deadlift followed by hip thrust.
Pre-exhaust supersets:	When you do a compound exercise set immediately followed by an isolation (single muscle) exercise set.
Post-exhaust supersets:	When you do an isolation exercise set immediately followed by a compound isolation set.

FACT: There are very few gluteal isolation exercises.

TRI SETS AND GIANT SETS

There are also tri sets and giant sets.

Tri-set – 3 exercises back to back.

Giant sets – 4 exercises back to back.

DROP SETS

This is used by many bodybuilders to increase muscle mass and muscular endurance. When performing an exercise, you immediately stop when your muscles are tired. However, you are only too tired to lift the weight you are using and you are not completely exhausted. When performing drop sets, once you are no longer able to continue lifting the heavier weight, immediately reduce or drop the weight and continue the set using a lighter weight until your muscles are fatigued again.

It is very difficult to use this method in the training program for working your booty because you wouldn't be able to take the weight off when you become fatigued when doing exercises such as barbell squats and glute bridges.

However, you could use drop sets in booty workouts when doing dumbbell squats. You would need all the dumbbells in front of you before you start. Another would be leg press, providing you had two spotters either side of the leg press machine to take a weight plate off once your muscles are tired and need to reduce the weight in order to continue.

An example of how a drop set would play out for dumbbell would be doing 10 reps using 35 pounds to failure, then dropping the weights to 8 reps using 27.5 pounds to failure, finishing with 6 reps using 25 pounds to failure.

TEMPO

This is to do with rep speed and is a measure of how quickly you move during a rep. An informative fact when you perform sets.

My programme will be using a 4-number code. Each number relates to the number of seconds for each rep you do. Using this system, every rep will be put into the 4 distinct phases/numbers of the code. Each number refers to the time in seconds it takes to complete each phase. However, not many exercises will follow the same code number in regards the amount of seconds it takes. See below.

Take for example, in a dumbbell stationary lunge

3 Eccentric > 1 Isometric > 1 Concentric > 1 Isometric > rep complete, next rep.

Therefore, to make it less complicated

3 seconds > 1 second > 1 second > 1 second

The 3>1>1>1 second code will not apply to every exercise you will perform. One example would be plyometric exercises as these are normally performed at very fast repetitions, especially during a bootcamp or HIIT class.

Another example would be if you were performing a barbell squat with a lot of added weight, especially the last rep! This is because it would take longer to squat back up to the starting position than it would if you were using little or no weight at all.

ECCENTRIC PHASE

This is when you lower the weight. For example, bending your legs to lunge when doing the dumbbell lunge.

HOLD BOTTOM

ISOMETRIC PHASE 1

This is a pause that separates eccentric and concentric phases. An example of this would be pausing at the bottom position when performing each rep of the dumbbell stationary lunge set. These pauses are very important for getting proper technique and controlled movement.

CONCENTRIC PHASE

This phase is the part of the movement where you lift (push or pull) the weight. For example, pushing through the legs to return to the starting position when performing the dumbbell lunge.

HOLD TOP

ISOMETRIC PHASE 2

This is a pause that separates eccentric and concentric phases. An example of this would be pausing at the top position after lunging back up to the starting position. These pauses are very important for contracting the target muscles.

REP SPEED

Normally you will start by moving slowly as you will have to consciously think about which body parts to move where. With practise, your technique will become more fluid and you will be able to move faster.

Once you have mastered an exercise technique, you will need to use an appropriate but challenging weight in order to prevent you from lifting too fast and potentially causing injury.

HOW AND WHEN TO PROGRESS WEIGHTS

You are ready to increase the weight when you can perform all of the desired repetitions on all sets and your technique is consistent from the first to last rep.

RIR NUMBER

This is short for REPETITIONS IN REVERSE. This technique was developed by a professional athlete and powerlifter called Michael Tuchscerer. RIR is where you note how many extra reps you can perform after achieving all of the desired repetitions of a set without struggle and in the correct form.

Let's say you were going to do 12 sumo deadlifts. If, after completing 12 reps with no struggle and proper technique, you were able to do a total of 14, then your RIR would be 2.

HOW TO ADJUST WITH THE RIR

If your RIR number was 1-2, then increase the weight by 5-10%. If it was 3 or more, then increase the weight by 10-15%.

WHEN TO USE THE RIR TEST

Use the test on your second or third set of an exercise if you can complete the target number of reps. The first set should be focused more on the correct posture and technique.

1 REP MAX (1RM)

This is when you monitor the heaviest weight you can lift with proper technique on just one rep. For example, if your sumo deadlift 1RM is 60kg, then using a weight that is 75% of your 1RM would be 45kg.

When you monitor your 1RM at the gym it's a good idea to do it on a separate day to your training days on the 38-session programme. This will definitely NOT affect any gains – in fact, it will probably increase your strength and allow you to lift heavier weights.

RPE SCALE

RPE stands for RATE of PERCEIVED EXERTION scale. This is used to record the intensity of an exercise.

The RPE scale is normally used for cardio, because you will be using SOME cardio, particularly on the warmup.

1-2 RPE = **Very easy.** Should feel like very little effort. But more than not moving at all.

3-4 RPE = **Easy.** This should feel like you can keep going at the pace for over an hour whilst being able to hold a full conversation.

5-6 RPE = **Moderate.** You will find it difficult to keep at this pace whilst holding a conversation. This should be starting to feel uncomfortable.

7-8 RPE = **Hard.** This pace should feel difficult to maintain and you will only be able to speak a few words.

9-10 RPE = **Maximum effort.** Almost impossible to keep going. You will be out of breath and unable to talk.

WHEN TO TRAIN

Consider when is the BEST time for you to train. When do you have the most energy? It must be based around your time and commitments.

ARE YOU GOING TO TRAIN:

First thing in the morning?

Before work?

Middle of the day?

After work?

Evenings?

FOR BEST RESULTS:

- Try to avoid training on 3 consecutive days to give your body time to recover.
- Train 3 of the workouts each week if you can. You can also hit the gym in addition if you have time so you can fit in an upper body workout, or a cardio workout such as spin or going for a swim.
- More importantly, keep on top of recovery (nutrition, sleep and stress). And do other things you enjoy! Ensure you are still socialising with your friends/ family and doing other activities, such as gardening, dancing, going for walks etc.

It's important that you follow the timetable I have given you. Each workout you do for my 38-session programme will be the MAIN WORKOUT. A key part of the workout is the warm up and the cool down. Do NOT skip it! (and remember that the flexibility exercises are just as important!)

WARM-UP

On this training programme, I give you all cardio as a warm-up.
Choose from any of the following to warm up:

Cross trainer

Treadmill

Stationary bike

Step machine

Rower

Recumbent bike

TIME SPENT ON WARM-UP

Too little warm up = less than 5 mins

Your muscles will be cold and sluggish and you are more likely to be distracted during the bulk of the workout.

Too much warm up = More than 10 mins

This will use up too much of the energy needed for the main part of the workout and you are likely to become fatigued too soon into the workout. Save some energy for building the booty!

The warm up should be between 5-10 minutes long.

Your body and muscles should feel warmed up and energised! If you feel like your body is all warmed up after 5 mins and you feel ready, it's probably a good time to get on with the next stage of the workout!

On the warm up, after 2 mins you should be at 5 on the RPE scale. This is so you are not exercising too intensely before you start the main section of the workout yet you are warming up your body.

COOL DOWN

This is a short amount of low intensity cardiovascular work after a workout.

It is important as it helps you to slowly return your breathing and heart rate to normal. If you stop exercising suddenly without taking the time to cool down, your heart rate slows abruptly and blood can pool in your lower body which can cause dizziness and even fainting.

For the cool down, choose a cardiovascular machine and spend 3 -5 mins on the exercise. On the RPE scale, you should be at a 3-4 (easy) to start with and come down to 1-2 (very easy).

KEEPING A WORKOUT JOURNAL

When you squat, bridge or deadlift heavy and achieve the desired amount of reps it is a fantastic feeling, especially if you achieve your target and beyond.

However, although you are more than likely able to remember how many reps with how much weight on one specific exercise you have achieved, it's very unlikely you will remember this for every exercise in your programme.

Recording your workouts can be highly motivational as it allows you to look back at the progress you make each week and set goals for future workouts. I am going to show you how to use a workout journal to record your workouts.

PREPARING YOUR JOURNAL

I prefer to use pen and paper as opposed to using my phone or tablet as I end up wasting too much time on Instagram! But if you can trust yourself not to get distracted, then choose to record your workout in a way that works best for you. But if you're like me and often get distracted, keep your phone in your gym locker!

From the start of the training programme, make sure you keep detailed records of your workouts. This will motivate you as you progress later in the training programme. I want you to focus on the main exercises that use weights and the aim is to increase the weight: such as squats, deadlifts, hip thrusts, glute bridges, lunges, etc.

Make sure you record every set with the amount of reps achieved, weight used, and whether you managed to complete all reps with the correct posture. Also, and importantly, ask yourself whether you could have completed more reps.

Let's say it's several weeks and sessions into the training programme. And today you are going to complete another workout.

Have a look at what exercises I have given you for the day. For example, if I have given you sumo deadlifts, go back to your previous sessions when you last did sumo deadlifts. Review how many reps you did, how much weight you used and whether you managed to complete all the reps with the correct posture.

Now you can use your previous achievements to set targets for the next workout I have given you on the training program.

Let's say, for example, at the previous session you managed 3 sets of sumo deadlifts. You used 20kg at each side of the bar (which equals 40kg in total) and you managed 10 reps with the correct posture on the first 2 sets, and you noted that you could've completed more. On the final set, you managed to complete 10 reps of 22.5kg on each side, which equals a total of 45kg.

Say I have given you 4 sets of 8 reps for your next workout. This is where the 1RM and RIR techniques come in. You could use the 1RM technique to calculate a prediction of how much weight you could use on 8 reps. The RIR method is for you to use if you achieved beyond 8 reps. If you achieved extra reps, then good! Now you know that you need to increase the weight – use the 1RM again to get down to 8 reps!

BY THE WAY, REMEMBER

1RM is 1 Rep Max when you note the heaviest weight you can lift with proper technique on just one rep

RIR is repetitions in reverse when you note how many extra reps you can perform after achieving the desired repetitions of a set without struggle and in proper form

If I have given you a flexible desired rep range – for example 8-12 reps – then this means you have the flexibility to choose the amount of reps you can do in the rep range. So, if you aimed for 9 reps and yet you achieved 11 reps, then you'd still be in the targeted rep range. You could do all sets at one specific rep range – such as 10 – or do a rep ladder going from 8 on the first set and then going up to 12. Alternatively, you could start at 12 reps and come down to 8. But still make note of the RIR method and whether you achieved the amount of reps with the correct posture.

RECORDING YOUR WORKOUT

After each set make sure you record the following:

- Amount of weight lifted
- Number of reps completed, plus the total amount of sets
- Whether you achieve the aimed reps with the correct form, and if you did, make a note if you could have achieved more reps with the correct technique/form.

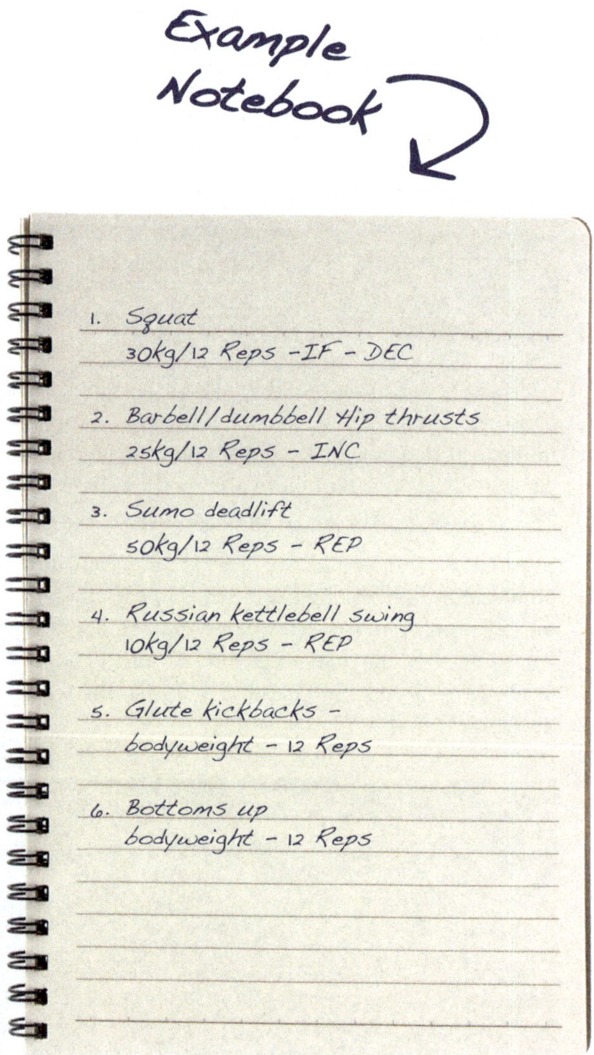

Use the following codes to monitor your performance and after every set:

IF = Incorrect form (unhappy with technique),

INC = Increase the weight next time,

DEC = Decrease weight next time,

REP = Same amount of weight next time.

MOOD STAGES – STAGE OF READINESS MODEL

The Stage of Readiness model identifies the process we go through when we are looking to change our behaviour and/or attitude, and want to step out of our comfort zones. There are 6 main stages, ranging from thinking about starting the Booty program to getting stuck into it like a bee in a flower. However, the model also reflects those times when we lose our willpower and don't give a F**k!

I designed the programme to make you avoid the latter and therefore I have added an extra phase – the Bite-back phase.

Here are the 7 phases:

PRE-CONTEMPLATION PHASE 1

This phase is when someone hasn't been thinking about exercise but has, for whatever reason, made the decision to make a change. In the booty building scenario, it could be seeing a picture of a naked model with the ass of your dreams that has given you the 'I want to wear that on top of mine' attitude. Or it could be standing naked in front of the mirror with a cup of coffee and asking yourself, 'Where did my ass go?' Or deciding 'I can do something with this booty!' Maybe you have seen an athlete, model, film star or pop star with the full lower body package of big, firm booty, defined legs, and sexy abs, and you have come to the conclusion that this booty programme can achieve this for you!

Another influence for the pre-contemplation phase is booking a holiday and trying on a bikini or sexy pair of Speedos and thinking, 'This looks hot but it needs a hot pair of cheeks to fill it!' Or even sexier, there could be a nude beach in your planned holiday destination, and the thought of wearing nothing but your new tan, giving a hot guy or girl something to have a cheeky look at as you make a refreshingly nude escape for a skinny dip gives you thrills! What could be sexier? And if you're single, you could feel you stand more chance of getting some holiday romance!

Maybe you've hit a milestone birthday and want to get that peachy ass just for you. Or perhaps you just want to give your partner something to hold onto! Whatever the reason, you have hit the pre-contemplation phase, you're in it and ready to take the next step.

CONTEMPLATION PHASE 2

This is where someone is contemplating taking action and is looking for a gym that suits their needs or thinking about making positive changes to their diet or lifestyle.

Maybe you have decided to eat clean for dinner by switching fries for sweet potato mash. Or you are going for a night out but switching beer for vodka and soda water. Or even when a mate asks you to go out partying, and you briefly pause and think, 'Hmm, maybe I shouldn't this once.' You may still go out, but the thought was there. The morning after you have the hangover from hell and think, 'Well, I really enjoyed myself buttttttttttttt...' Yep, you are on your way through to the next phase!

PREPARATION/PLANNING PHASE 3

OK, so your attitude has changed quite a lot already. At this stage, you are seeking resources for the road ahead! This will involve shopping around for a gym that fulfils your needs but is within your budget, and/or signing up for fitness classes to get your motivation started as it is likely your motivation and confidence are still missing to an extent. Or you may even be shopping for gym clothes that make you look cute and quirky in the gym, but even sexier for when your booty gets even more beautiful

Your confidence and behaviour still isn't 100% there but you are ready to make a brave CHANGE! And it will change even more once you enter the gym for your first session!

ACTION PHASE 4

In action phase you are READY for ACTION – pretty obvious, right! You may be hitting the treadmill, taking part in your first fitness class such as HIIT, insanity, spin or even pilates. Alternatively, you could be trying a few weights and joining in a mini workout with a new buddy you've met in the gym.

Warning: This is a phase where some people slip out for many reasons and go back to before square one! To be fair, there are reasons beyond our control that could cause this to happen. However, many of these reasons are when our mindsets and willpower clash with something. This could be that you see a person in your gym every day who looks amazing, yet you feel you look like s**t when you stand next to them in the weights section. Or you could have one or more bad sessions where you feel you embarrassed yourself, let yourself down or underachieved.

DON'T let this happen. The day you give up is likely the day before you excelled at the gym. That day would lead to another day, and before you know if you would have built enough momentum to see significant results because you stayed at it 3 times a week for several months and kept a routine. You would also start to make vital and handy routine habits. Instead of purchasing a protein flapjack after every workout, you decide it would be cheaper to buy a pack of 10 and save money, 'since I'm gonna stick at this for a while!' Once you have started and settled into your essential routines, you are shaking your ass through to the next stage!

MAINTENANCE PHASE 5

You have made a significant change and, even better, you are maintaining the change in your new behaviour. In most cases, this phase happens about 6 months from the beginning of the action phase. Anyway, the action has been done. If you are at this stage, give yourself a cheeky pat on your ass! You are achieving goals you did not expect to achieve – maybe you are squatting twice as heavy as you ever expected to, or you have changed your twice a week visit to the kebab shop to once a month! You may at times not want to visit the gym, yet you would NOT dare to skip it as you want to achieve your goals and know you would regret it far more in the morning.

It's believed that if you train regularly at the gym for more than 6 months, your goals and new lifestyle/ways have become ingrained. You NEED to maintain this because the next stage is kind of depressing.

RELAPSE PHASE 6

This is not ideal but common. This is where you could be going to the gym a bit less and it goes downhill from there. Why could this be? Your boyfriend purchased Netflix and you think, 'I wanna watch this'? But this has clashed with your gym habits and your routine has changed in favour of your TV and chillin'. Because you are making it to the gym less often, you are less motivated, more distracted, not performing quite as well and your new habits go from bad to worse.

Coming back after a holiday is a typical form of relapse – it's happened to me! We decide to let our hair down, party hard, eat and drink what and when we want, and wake up and go to sleep when we want. When we return home, having the holiday blues is one of many barriers to getting back into our daily, healthy routines. If we have been on an international vacation, there is also the jet lag we have to deal with, which can last weeks! Motivation very easily goes out of the window. When I last came back from the US, the first thing I wanted to do when I got back home was prepare a cocktail with the recipe the bartender gave me on vacation and make my own dirty fries.

Of course, there are many other unfortunate circumstances that cause a relapse, when going to the gym or sticking to a diet just isn't on our minds in the slightest. This could be losing your job, becoming unwell for a period of time, or even a death in the family.

Relapse typically occurs during the action or maintenance phase. It happens. If you feel you are in this phase, then don't beat yourself up. But dust yourself off and get back into the swing of it to achieve your booty goals. You need your mindset back in the game!

Relapse can happen for just a few weeks if you haven't felt 100% and your mind wanted a staycation for a recovery week, or you were stressed after a change of circumstances and needed some 'me' time. On the other hand, a relapse could start by thinking, 'Nah, a few weeks off then I'm back into it', and weeks become MONTHS. And months become YEARS!

Getting back into the gym after a lengthy relapse phase may be very daunting but you must think short term pain, long term gain!

Also remember that setting a goal to beat your previous gain is such a rewarding achievement!

If you consider yourself in the relapse phase, think of the success you had whilst in the maintenance phase. You were THE person – or close to being the person – you wanted to be.

TIP: Relapse is a normal part of behavioural change.

TIP: You have not lost until you have truly given up!

TIP: If you have got yourself into the maintenance phase, you can do it again!

BITE-BACK PHASE 7

Now this is where you BITE BACK! I gave you a pep-talk at the end of the relapse phase, but now I will get you out of it and back on it like a car bonnet!

So if you do consider yourself in relapse, the aim is you get you back into action, ideally as soon as possible.

Refrain from negative self-talk. Many people believe they will never look or feel as good as they did in the past. Unless something very drastic happened, such as a tragic accident, you always have the opportunity to get back to what you were.

Maybe you are being too hard on yourself. Remember, it is common to relapse, especially if you have not relapsed before. No-one is perfect; many celebrities go through infamous relapse stages and unfortunately the media is unfairly harsh on them.

Think of any barriers that caused or helped trigger the relapse. Write them down and divide them into 3 sections: PERSONAL, FAMILY/SOCIAL and ENVIRONMENTAL. To give you an idea of what would go under each category, here are some examples:

Personal
Lack of time; self-doubt; low energy; low motivation; non-enjoyment of fitness; the gym being too daunting, crap or simply 'not nice to be in'; cost; being uncomfortable around strangers; or it could be very personal, such as illness or injury.

Family/social
Childcare; looking after a poorly family member or friend; having a lack of time with your friends so you have to choose gym vs social life; another hobby takes up too much of your spare time; family events such as a Sunday gathering.

Environmental
Insufficent public transport to get to a gym; constant traffic during hours you are free to go to the gym; the weather being too bad if you usually cycle to the gym.

For each barrier, figure out:

- Can I change this?'
- Do I need help to change it?

And more importantly,

- Am I willing to change it?

If a barrier you listed in any of those columns scored a NO in 'Can I change this?' then it cannot be helped. But if it scores a YES, YOU have the power to change it.

Seek help. You don't have to do this alone. Do you think you would benefit from a personal trainer to get you back into your maintenance phase? If you have the disposable income for it, then it's definitely worth it if it will help you. If a fitness instructor is not occupied with another customer while you are back at the gym, you are within your rights to ask for any sort of help. You may not have done a barbell squat in months and months, but it's perfectly OK to ask a member of staff to check you are doing it in the correct form.

Do you think you need any sort of emotional help to take you out of your relapse? I am not a counsellor but if you feel you need any sort of help, such as counselling, cognitive behavioural therapy or maybe you just want to talk to a specialist, then it's not a weakness to seek professional help. In fact, it shows strength and will do you no end of good. Not just for your fitness goals but for your family's and loved ones' happiness as well as your own.

Can childcare be sorted out? Does your son or daughter attend a club that gives you the free time to sneak to the gym for an hour or so — maybe there is a playcare section at the gym? Or can a family member look after them a certain day of the week? Do your kids have friends whose parents also enjoy the gym? Maybe you could take turns e.g. you have their kids one day so they can go to the gym and then another day they have your kids so you are free for the gym. This could also improve your child's social life!

Is there a friend you could buddy up with and train together? If there was to be a second relapse, one of you could help the other get out of it quickly.

And here's a special booty building workout programme technique for you!

There's nothing cuter than a little puppy or a kitten, right? So let's say someone came along and said, "A little puppy/kitten has been kidnapped and they are crying in the woods, waiting for you to go and rescue them!" You're gonna go and rescue them, of course! Well, I would, as I'm a massive animal lover. (Dogs over kids anyway for me!) Imagine that each session in the gym takes you a step closer to rescuing that adorable animal who is waiting for you. Perhaps set yourself a target that 38 sessions gets you next to that adorable fluffball and they jump into your arms!

If you're not an animal lover, imagine a peach emoji with a cute, smiley face sending you hugs over your laptop or phone. Sounds cute! Now imagine it has a happy little baby peach next to it. But next time you look at the screen, the peach emoji is crying, and the poor little thing is being dissolved. You believe you are never going to see it again!

Your screen shows a message saying the peach has been sent to the emoji jail and to get it back you need to adopt it. To adopt it you have to complete the 38-session programme. Then it will be back in your arms. Now relate this back to the puppy and kitten example. Of course you can't compare an emoji to a puppy or a kitten, but do you see where I'm coming from?

Yes, this is a quirky way of motivating yourself but the last thing I wanted was for this book to be normal!

HOW TO BITE BACK!

Buddy up with a friend – they could have booty goals.

Have a picture of future holiday destinations on your fridge.

Look for new clothes that you normally would think are too revealing.

Make your own weekly schedule by deciding which days you can go to the gym and which are your rest days.

Look for pictures of booties on the internet. A great form of inspiration!

If it's not too cold, walk around in your swimsuit at home!

If you start the 38-week Booty Building programme and consider yourself in RELAPSE mode, but have overcome it and you are now biting back and back in ACTION, then it is probably a good idea to invest a week refreshing and familiarising yourself with all the exercises involved in the programme that you were doing prior to relapse. Review your workout journal and remind yourself of where you got to. Again, don't feel embarrassed or think that you're a pain in the ass if you need an instructor or someone else in the gym to watch your body position and technique whilst executing the exercises.

Get on it!

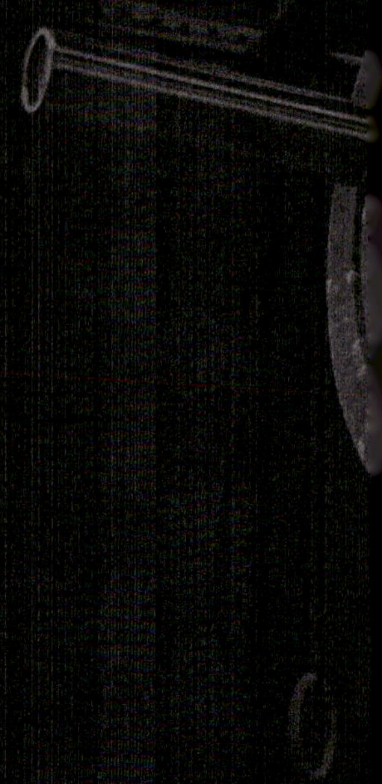

NOW IT'S TIME FOR THE 38-SESSION PROGRAMME

THINGS TO REMEMBER BEFORE YOU GET GOING

01 Remember the RIR method! Don't hesitate to use it at any time or rep. For example, if you are aiming to do 4 sets of 10 reps, but you can easily do 10 reps, then go beyond and experiment with the RIR method. Then you can increase the weight and aim for 10. The rep range is just the aim I have given you. Don't be restricted by it.

02 If you can't achieve the amount of reps I have asked for, don't worry. It's an aim at the end of the day! Decrease the weight on the next set.

03 If you feel you will need a spotter on higher risk exercises such as barbell squat or leg press, be safe rather than sorry. Spotters can increase confidence levels, which pushes you to lift heavier weights. And if you are struggling, they can help you when you are in any sort of danger if you were to take too much weight or reps on!

04 The amount of work I have asked you to do may seem a lot to achieve in an hour's time slot, but if you keep the rest periods between sets at a minute or 90 seconds it can be done.

If you have been doing the workout for more than an hour and not quite finished, go straight to the cool down and end flexibility. This is so you don't over-train.

05 Don't push yourself too hard. If you feel pain, shortness of breath, dizziness, nausea or if you feel sick, take a break. If you still feel the same after the break, it's probably best to call it a day and start the workout again on a day you feel better.

06 Make sure you are well hydrated and take enough water with you to the gym. Dehydration can strongly affect a person's ability to train at their highest potential.

07 Don't forget to eat! Your body needs energy and you should eat before exercising so your body has enough fuel to power through your workout.

If you are going to eat 2 to 3 hours before a workout, then have a full meal high in complex carbs, fats and lean protein. This should have of at least 400 calories to fuel the body. If you are taller and more muscular, then you will probably need even more calories.

If you have got an hour to spare before hitting the gym, then have a snack which prioritises carbs (approximately 40 grams) with some protein as your meal source. An ideal snack would be some granola with a small scoop of protein powder and milk.

If you have less than an hour, choose a simple but healthy snack that has approximately 20 grams of carbs. You will need something easy to digest if you are lifting shortly after!

08 Don't forget to eat after working out as well. If you want your glutes to get bigger you will need a snack of a 2:1 ratio minimum carbs:protein. If you just want to be lean and more defined in the booty whilst having a calorie deficit, then a 1:1 ratio would be appropriate.

09 Make the most of using your workout journal.

10 Very important! Go into the gym in the right mindset! If you are feeling like s#×t for whatever reason, take deep breaths and try to get yourself in a better frame of mind. It's very likely you'll not perform as well if you are in a crappy mood or if you've got a bee in your bonnet. Once you've given yourself time to calm down and cheer up, get going and smash your workout! You'll notice a big boost in your mood.

11 Again, consult with your doctor if you feel any outlining health conditions that should be taken into consideration in regards to the 38-session programme.

So when you're ready, **GET GOING! YOU CAN DO THIS!**

WORKOUT ORDER

WARM UP

PRE-FLEXIBILITY

MAIN WORKOUT

COOL DOWN

POST-FLEXIBILITY

DONE!

EXAMPLE WORKOUT

WARM UP

Cross trainer 5 minutes

PRE-FLEXIBILITY

MAIN WORKOUT

1. **Bodyweight squat 1 set of 20 reps**
2. **Superset – Hip thrust/goblet squat**
   3 sets of supersets
   Barbell/ dumbbell hip thrusts 10-15 reps
   Goblet squat 10 - 15 reps
3. **Sumo deadlift 3 sets of 10 reps**
4. **Russian kettlebell swing 3 sets of 10-15 reps**
5. **Glute kickbacks 3 sets of 20 reps**
   (alternate each leg so it's 10 reps on each leg)

COOLDOWN

POST-FLEXIBILITY

THE THREE MAIN WORKOUT PHASES

I have divided the 38-session programme into 3 phases:

PHASE 01 SESSIONS 1 – 12

This is the first and most scary phase but hopefully you will be 'well into it' after this phase is done. Gains will slowly be on their way and you may already feel a difference!

PHASE 02 SESSIONS 13 – 25

You might think 'God, I'm only a third of the way through' but this phase is where you will really start to see gains, and by the end of this phase you've only got a third to go!

PHASE 03 SESSIONS 26 – 38

You will be feeling proud and seeing major differences. (Obvs, I can't guarantee!) You should be really determined to finally get this intense programme completed. Bitch, you are almost done!

PHASE 01 SESSIONS 1-12

This is by far the scariest stage of the three phases. I have been there myself as I once did a 12-week programme designed by Jay Cutler and I know how scary it can be. Remember that practice makes perfect and it's never a bad time to double check anything.

The early stage in your programme is an ideal opportunity for you make notes and record in your workout journal about your first achieved lifts, at what weight, and how many successful repetitions in the correct form. You could also take some pictures of yourself before your first session. This will give you an extra bit of motivation for your before and after pics!

As you come near the end of phase 1, note more recordings in your journal and set some targets for the same stage of phase 2. Don't be at all disappointed with yourself if you don't quite achieve them!

It may seem like you have a long way to go, but ENJOY it. If you are struggling, then remember, **SHORT TERM PAIN, LONG TERM GAIN.**

WORKOUT 01

WARM UP

PRE-FLEXIBILITY

MAIN WORKOUT

1. Bodyweight squat 1 set of 20 reps
2. Superset – Hip thrust/Goblet squat
   3 sets of supersets
   Barbell/dumbbell hip thrusts 10-15 reps
   Goblet squat 10-15 reps
3. Sumo deadlift 4 sets of 10 reps
4. Russian kettlebell swing 3 sets of 10-15 reps
5. Glute kickbacks
   3 sets of 10-15 reps on each leg
6. Bottoms up 3 sets of 1 minute intervals
   30-second rest in between sets

COOLDOWN

POST-FLEXIBILITY

WORKOUT 02

WARM UP

PRE-FLEXIBILITY

MAIN WORKOUT

1. **Bird dog** 2 sets of 15 reps on each leg
2. **Bodyweight box step-ups** 1 set of 12-20 reps
   Alternate with which leg you step up with
3. **Dumbbell box step-ups** 3 sets of 10-20 reps
   Alternate with which leg you step up with
4. **Bodyweight reverse lunge** 2 sets of 12-20 reps
   Alternate with each leg you come back with
5. **Dumbbell reverse lunge** 4 sets of 10-15 reps
   Alternate with each leg you come back with
6. **Barbell glute bridge** 4 sets of 10-15 reps
   Pause for 2 seconds at the top after every rep
7. **Box jumps** 3 sets of 8 -12 reps. Or until failure

COOLDOWN

POST-FLEXIBILITY

WORKOUT 03

WARM UP

PRE-FLEXIBILITY

MAIN WORKOUT

1. **Burpees** 2 sets of 12-15 reps
2. **Barbell squat (just the bar)** 1 set of 15-20 reps
3. **Barbell squat pyramid sets**
   1st – 15 reps
   2nd – 12 reps
   3rd – 9 reps
   4th – 12 reps
   5th – 15 reps
4. **Squat jumps** 4 sets of 12-15 reps or until failure
5. **Scorpion kicks** 6 sets of 12-15 reps (3 on each leg)
6. **Superset – Side-lying abduction/Side plank**
   4 sets of supersets – 2 on each side
   Side-lying abduction 10-20 reps
   Side plank 30 seconds

COOLDOWN

POST-FLEXIBILITY

WORKOUT 04

WARM UP

PRE-FLEXIBILITY

MAIN WORKOUT

1. Froggers 2 sets of 20 reps (alternate each leg)
2. Leg Press 6 sets of 8-12 reps
3. Superset – Dumbbell lateral lunge/pull through with cable
   4 sets of supersets
   Dumbbell lateral lunge 12 reps – alternate each leg
   Cable pull through 8-12 reps
4. Superset – Bodyweight incline glute bridge/Plank
   3 sets of supersets
   Bodyweight incline glute bridge 10-15 reps
   Plank 45 seconds
5. Bicycle crunches 4 sets of 45 seconds

COOLDOWN

POST-FLEXIBILITY

WORKOUT 05

WARM UP

PRE-FLEXIBILITY

MAIN WORKOUT

1. **Thrusters off the box** 2 sets of 15 reps
2. **Romanian deadlift** 5 sets of 8-12 reps
3. **Front barbell squat** 5 sets of 8-12 reps
4. **Mountain climbers** 3 sets of 45 seconds
5. **Firearms** 4 sets of 15 reps – 2 sets on each leg
6. **Reverse crunches** 3 sets until failure

COOLDOWN

POST-FLEXIBILITY

WORKOUT 06

WARM UP

PRE-FLEXIBILITY

MAIN WORKOUT

1. **Bird dog** 2 sets of 20 reps
2. **Single-legged squat bodyweight or with kettlebell**
   3 sets of 6-12 reps on each leg or until failure
3. **Superset – Stiff-legged deadlift/Bodyweight glute bridge**
   4 sets of supersets
   Stiff-legged deadlift 6-12 reps
   Bodyweight glute bridge
   12 reps, followed by a 10-second hold
4. **Superset – Sumo deadlift/Bodyweight hip thrust**
   3 sets of supersets
   Sumo deadlift 6-12 reps
   Bodyweight hip thrust 12 reps
5. **Squat Jumps** 4 sets of 30-second intervals
   30-second rest in between
6. **Basic crunches** 3 sets until failure

COOLDOWN

POST-FLEXIBILITY

WORKOUT 07

WARM UP

PRE-FLEXIBILITY

MAIN WORKOUT

1. Lunge walk from one side of the room and side-walk squat back 2 sets. 1 bodyweight – 1 with kettlebell

2. Barbell squat warm up with just the bar or with light weights 1 set – 15-20 reps

3. Pyramids – Barbell squat 7 sets in total
   12 reps – 10 reps – 8 reps
   6 reps – 8 reps – 10 reps – 12 reps

4. Superset – Box jumps/Box step-downs
   3 sets of supersets
   Box jumps 12 reps
   Box step-downs 12 reps. 6 reps on each leg

5. Plank 2 sets of 90 seconds or until failure

6. Bottoms up 2 sets of 1 minute intervals

COOLDOWN

POST-FLEXIBILITY

WORKOUT 08

WARM UP

PRE-FLEXIBILITY

MAIN WORKOUT

1. **Bodyweight or goblet squat with light weight**
   2 sets of 12-20 reps
2. **Bulgarian split squat bodyweight or with a kettlebell**
   8-12 reps. 3 sets on each leg
3. **Stationary lunge with dumbbells**
   2 sets of 8-12 reps on each leg
4. **One-legged glute bridge** 2 sets of 12-15 reps on each leg
5. **Scorpion kicks** 2 sets of 12-15 reps on each leg
6. **Superset – Side-lying abduction leg raise/Side plank**
   2 sets on each side
   Lying abduction leg raise 12 reps
   Side plank 30-second hold

COOLDOWN

POST-FLEXIBILITY

WORKOUT 09

WARM UP

PRE-FLEXIBILITY

MAIN WORKOUT

1. **Forward jump squats to one side of the room and bodyweight walking lunge back to the start**
   2 sets from one side of the room to the other

2. **Superset – Conventional deadlift/Russian kettlebell swing**
   4 sets of supersets
   Conventional deadlift 8-10 reps
   Russian kettlebell swing 10 reps

3. **Superset – Barbell hip thrust/Russian kettlebell swing** 4 sets
   Barbell hip thrusts 8-10 reps
   Russian kettlebell swings 10 reps

4. **Hyperextensions** 4 sets of 10-15 reps

5. **Firearms** 2 sets of 15 reps on each leg

6. **Superset – Scorpion kick/ Scorpion kick pulse**
   2 sets of supersets on each leg
   Scorpion kicks 12 reps
   Scorpion kick pulses 10 pulses

COOLDOWN

POST-FLEXIBILITY

WORKOUT 10

WARM UP

PRE-FLEXIBILITY

MAIN WORKOUT

1. **Mountain climbers** 3 sets of 45-second intervals, 30-second rest in between
2. **Superset – Hack squat/Wall squat hold** 4 sets of supersets
   Hack squat 6 -12 reps **Wall squat** 30-second hold
3. **Superset – Barbell glute bridge/ Bodyweight glute bridge hold** 4 sets of supersets
   Barbell glute bridge
   4 sets of 10-12 reps with a 3-second hold after every rep
   Bodyweight glute bridge hold 20 seconds
4. **Superset – Dumbbell between platform squat/ Bodyweight glute bridge pulse**
   3 sets of supersets
   Dumbbell between platform squat 8-12 reps
   Bodyweight glute bridge pulse 20 seconds
5. **Lunge jumps** 5 sets of 30-second intervals
   30-second rest in between sets
6. **Superset – Bottoms up/Reverse crunches**
   3 sets of superset intervals
   Bottoms up 45 seconds
   Reverse crunches 45 seconds

COOLDOWN

POST-FLEXIBILITY

WORKOUT 11

WARM UP

PRE-FLEXIBILITY

MAIN WORKOUT

1. **Bodyweight forward lunge**
   2 sets of 12 reps. 2 sets on each leg
2. **Sumo deadlift with just the bar or with light weight or a kettlebell** 1 set of 15–20 reps
3. **Pyramids – Sumo deadlifts** 7 sets in total
   15 reps – 12 reps – 9 reps – 6 reps
   9 reps – 12 rep – 15 reps
4. **Superset – Dumbbell squat/Mason twist**
   3 sets of supersets
   Dumbbell squat 8–10 reps
   Mason twist 20-second intervals
5. **Plank** 4 sets
   50-second intervals. 20-second rest in between sets
6. **Mason twists** 3 sets of 45-second intervals
   20-second rest in between sets

COOLDOWN

POST-FLEXIBILITY

WORKOUT 12

WARM UP

PRE-FLEXIBILITY

MAIN WORKOUT

1. **Bodyweight calf-raised glute bridge** 2 sets of 16 reps
2. **Barbell squat – Just the bar or light weight added**
   1 set of 15-20 reps
3. **Superset – Barbell squat/Bodyweight glute bridge**
   4 sets of supersets
   Barbell squat 6-10 reps
   Bodyweight glute bridge
   12 reps and add a 10-second hold after
4. **Barbell hip thrust** 4 sets of 8-12 reps
5. **Superset – Reverse crunch/Basic crunch**
   4 sets of supersets
   Reverse crunch 45 seconds
   Basic crunch 45 seconds
6. **Superset – Scorpion kick/Scorpion kick pulse**
   2 sets of supersets on each leg
   Scorpion kicks 12 reps
   Scorpion kick pulses 10 pulses

COOLDOWN

POST-FLEXIBILITY

PHASE 02 SESSIONS 13–25

At this stage, you may still be slightly anxious as you are still less than halfway through. You could also be feeling very good about yourself and feel as if you have got your feet under the table with the programme. You more than likely will already see a reasonable amount of gains, and remember it is YOU who has worked for it.

Take new notes and recordings in your workout journal, and compare your results to when you started in Phase 1. How much have you progressed? Again, set yourself new goals but don't be too disappointed if you don't achieve them as it's easy to be over-ambitious – and quite frankly, there's nothing wrong with that! You are doing so well. Keep up your hard work and DONT GIVE UP!

WORKOUT 13

WARM UP

PRE-FLEXIBILITY

MAIN WORKOUT

1. **Bird dog** 1 set of 20 reps. Alternate each leg
2. **Conventional deadlift** 1 set of 20 reps
   Warm up with just the bar or light amount of weight.
3. **Pyramids – Conventional deadlifts**
   15 reps – 12 reps – 9 reps – 12 reps – 15 reps
4. **Barbell Reverse lunge with just the bar** 1 set of 20 reps
   Alternate each leg you come back with so you do 10 reps on each leg
5. **Barbell reverse lunge** 3 sets of 12 reps
   Alternate each leg you come back with so you do 6 reps on each leg
6. **Double-quadrupled hip abduction**
   3 sets of 12 reps on each side/leg
7. **Bottoms up** 4 sets of 1 minute intervals
   30-second rest in between sets

COOLDOWN

POST-FLEXIBILITY

WORKOUT 14

WARM UP

PRE-FLEXIBILITY

MAIN WORKOUT

1. Mountain climbers 3 sets of 45-second intervals, 30-second rest in between
2. Superset – Dumbbell hip thrust/ Bodyweight crab hip thrust pulse
   4 sets of supersets
   Dumbbell hip thrust 12-15 reps. 3-second hold on every rep
   Bodyweight crab hip thrust pulse
   12 pulses plus a 10-second hold after
3. Superset – Dumbbell glute bridge/ Bodyweight glute bridge pulse
   4 sets of supersets
   Dumbbell glute bridge 12-15 reps. 3-second hold on every rep
   Bodyweight glute bridge pulse
   12 pulses plus a 10-second hold after
4. Superset – Side-lying hip raise/Side-lying hip abduction
   3 sets on each side
   Side-lying hip raise 12 reps
   Side-lying hip abduction 12 reps
5. Firearms 3 sets of 12-15 reps on each side
6. V-sit crunches
   3 sets of 45 seconds intervals. 20-second rest between sets

COOLDOWN

POST-FLEXIBILITY

WORKOUT 15

WARM UP

PRE-FLEXIBILITY

MAIN WORKOUT

1. **Bodyweight forward lunge**
   1 set of 15 reps on each side. 2 in total
2. **Bodyweight reverse lunge**
   1 set of 15 reps on each side. 2 in total
3. **Barbell squat** 5 sets of 6-10 reps
4. **Conventional deadlift** 4 sets of 8-12 reps
5. **Lunge jumps** 4 sets of 45-second intervals
6. **Forearm plank up to plank on your palms, then back down**
   2 sets of 45-second intervals.
   20-second rest in between sets

COOLDOWN

POST-FLEXIBILITY

WORKOUT 16

WARM UP

PRE-FLEXIBILITY

MAIN WORKOUT

1. **Bodyweight lateral lunge**
   2 sets of 16 reps. 8 reps on each side
2. **Leg press with little or no added weight**
   1 set of 15-20 reps
3. **Pyramids – Leg Press**
   15 reps – 12 reps – 9 reps – 6 reps – 9 reps
   12 reps – 15 reps
4. **Lateral lunge with dumbbells**
   3 sets of 10-12 reps
5. **Box step-ups with dumbbells** 4 sets of 20 reps
   Alternate each leg you go up with
6. **Superset – Basic crunch/Mason twist**
   4 sets of supersets. 30-second rest between supersets
   Basic crunch 30 seconds
   Mason twist 30 seconds

COOLDOWN

POST-FLEXIBILITY

WORKOUT 17

WARM UP

PRE-FLEXIBILITY

MAIN WORKOUT

1. Bodyweight glute bridge 1 set of 15-20 reps
2. Stiff-legged deadlift with just the bar or low weight added
   1 set of 20 reps
3. Stiff-legged deadlift 4 sets of 10-12 reps
4. Superset – Barbell box squat/Dumbbell hip thrust
   5 sets of supersets
   Barbell box squat 10 reps
   Dumbbell hip thrust 10-15 reps
5. Mountain climbers
   4 sets of 45-second intervals. 30-second rest in between.
6. Superset – Mason twist/Reverse crunch
   30-second rest in between supersets
   3 sets of supersets
   Mason twist 30 seconds
   Reverse crunch 30 seconds

COOLDOWN

POST-FLEXIBILITY

WORKOUT 18

WARM UP

PRE-FLEXIBILITY

MAIN WORKOUT

1. **Bottoms up** 2 sets of 15 reps
2. **Squat jumps** 3 sets of 15 reps
3. **Box jumps** 3 sets of 12 reps
4. **Reverse lunge to box step-ups** 2 sets of 12 reps
   Alternate each leg you lunge back and step up with
5. **Cable pull through** 3 sets of 12-15 reps
6. **Superset - Scorpion kick/ Scorpion kick pulse**
   3 sets on each leg
   Scorpion kick 12 reps
   Scorpion kick pulse 12 pulses
7. **Superset – Reverse crunch/Basic crunch**
   2 sets of a combined 2-minute intervals
   1 minute rest between supersets
   Reverse crunch 1 minute
   Basic crunch 1 minute

COOLDOWN

POST-FLEXIBILITY

WORKOUT 19

WARM UP

PRE-FLEXIBILITY

MAIN WORKOUT

1. **Box squat** 2 sets of 15 reps
2. **Single-leg squats bodyweight or with a light kettlebell**
   2 sets of a maximum of 10 reps on each leg
3. **Barbell glute bridge** 5 sets of 8-12 reps
4. **Superset – Wall squat/Russian kettlebell swing**
   3 sets of supersets
   Wall squat 45-second intervals
   Russian kettlebell swing 12-15 reps
5. **Superset – Kettlebell box squat/Incline glute bridge**
   3 sets of supersets
   Kettlebell box squats 12 reps
   Hold the weight as if you were doing a goblet squat
   Incline glute bridge 12-15 reps
6. **Pyramids – Plank**
   30 seconds
   45 seconds
   1 minute
   45 seconds
   30 seconds

COOLDOWN

POST-FLEXIBILITY

WORKOUT 20

WARM UP

PRE-FLEXIBILITY

MAIN WORKOUT

1. **Burpees** 2 sets of 15 reps
2. **Leg press** with no or little weight. Neutral leg stance
   1 set of 15-20 reps
3. **Leg press** Neutral leg stance
   3 sets of 8-12 reps
4. **Leg press.** Higher leg stance
   3 sets of 8-12 reps
5. **Stationary lunge with dumbbells**
   3 sets of 10-12 reps on each leg
6. **Bottoms up**
   3 sets of 45-second intervals
   30-second rest in between sets

COOLDOWN

POST-FLEXIBILITY

WORKOUT 21

WARM UP

PRE-FLEXIBILITY

MAIN WORKOUT

1. **Bodyweight reverse lunge**
   2 sets of 20 reps
   Alternate each leg you come back with so you're doing 10 lunges on each set on each leg.
2. **Bodyweight single-legged squat**
   1 set of 15-20 reps on each side/leg
3. **Single-legged squat with dumbbells**
   3 sets of 8-12 reps on each side/leg
4. **Bulgarian split squat with kettlebell**
   3 sets of 8-12 reps on each leg
5. **Superset – Dumbbell glute bridge/Bicycle crunches**
   4 sets of supersets
   Dumbbell glute bridge 10-12 reps
   Bicycle crunches 45-second intervals
6. **Basic crunch 4 sets of 15 reps**

COOLDOWN

POST-FLEXIBILITY

WORKOUT 22

WARM UP

PRE-FLEXIBILITY

MAIN WORKOUT

1. **Bodyweight curtsy lunge** **2 sets of 14 reps**
   Alternate each leg you come out with on every rep
2. **Barbell squat – Low to light added weight**
   1 set of 20 reps
3. **Pyramids – Barbell squat**
   12 reps – 10 reps – 8 reps – 6 reps
   8 reps – 10 reps – 12 reps
4. **Superset – Side-lying hip abduction/Side plank hold**
   3 supersets on each side
   Execute both exercises of the superset on the same side your body is positioned.

   Side-lying hip abduction **15 reps**
   Side plank hold **30 seconds**
5. **Side-lying hip raise** **2 sets of 15 reps on each side/leg**
6. **Superset – Crab hip thrust/Reverse crunch**
   2 supersets of 45 seconds on each exercise

COOLDOWN

POST-FLEXIBILITY

WORKOUT 23

WARM UP

PRE-FLEXIBILITY

MAIN WORKOUT

1. **Bodyweight stationary lunge**
   1 set of 12-20 reps on each leg/side. 2 sets in total
2. **Conventional deadlift with just the bar or light added weight**
   1 set of 20 reps
3. **Pyramids – Conventional deadlift**
   12 reps – 10 reps – 8 reps – 6 reps
   8 reps – 10 reps – 12 reps
4. **Double quadrupled hip abduction**
   2 sets of 12-15 reps on each side/leg
5. **Superset – Scorpion kick**
   & Fire hydrant/Scorpion kick pulse
   2 supersets of 30-second intervals on both exercises on each side/leg. 30-second rest in between sets.

   On the first exercise, do a Scorpion kick and then do a Fire hydrant. Remain doing the exercise on this leg/side for 30 seconds and then do the Scorpion kick pulse on the same leg. Then do the same on the opposite leg.

COOLDOWN

POST-FLEXIBILITY

WORKOUT 24

WARM UP

PRE-FLEXIBILITY

MAIN WORKOUT

1. **Bird dog** 2 sets of 20 reps
2. **Superset – Jump squats/Mason twist**
   4 supersets of 30-second intervals on each exercise.
3. **Superset – Lunge jumps/Mountain climbers**
   4 supersets of 30-second intervals on each exercise.
4. **Superset – Wall squat/ Plank**
   4 supersets of 30-second intervals on each exercise.
5. **Superset – Side-lying hip raise/Side Plank**
   2 supersets on each side/leg
   Once you have done the side-lying hip raise, do the side plank on the same side/leg

   Side lying hip raise 12-15 reps
   Side plank 30-second hold
6. **Reverse crunches**
   Intervals of 45 seconds on, 15 seconds off for 5 minutes

COOLDOWN

POST-FLEXIBILITY

WORKOUT 25

WARM UP

PRE-FLEXIBILITY

MAIN WORKOUT

1. **Bodyweight or goblet squat with light weight**
   2 sets of 12-20 reps
2. **Barbell Bulgarian split squat 3 sets on each leg. 8-12 reps**
3. **Stationary lunge with dumbbells**
   2 sets of 8-12 reps on each leg
4. **Superset – One-legged glute bridge/**
   One-legged glute bridge pulse
   2 supersets on each leg
   One-legged glute bridge 12-15 reps
   One-legged glute bridge pulse 10 pulses
5. **Superset – Scorpion kick**
   & Fire hydrant/Scorpion kick pulse.
   2 supersets of 30-second intervals on both exercises on each side/leg. 30-second rest in between sets.

   On the first exercise, do a Scorpion kick and then do a Fire hydrant. Remain doing the exercise on this leg/side for 30 seconds and then do the Scorpion kick pulse on the same leg. Then do the same on the opposite leg.

COOLDOWN

POST-FLEXIBILITY

PHASE 03 SESSIONS 26–38

Almost there! You should be very proud of what you have accomplished. Bear in mind, no matter how long you have been working out for, it's always a good idea to check your posture from time to time.

YOU'VE GOT THIS!

As you near the end of Phase 3, record more gains in your workout journal and look back at phases 1 and 2. Even if you don't achieve your goals, don't worry as it's not necessarily about hitting them! It's about giving you the drive and self-motivation to push yourself and progress mentally and physically.

Stay determined and focused by setting yourself new goals for once you have finished Phase 3 and you are ready to go at it alone.

WORKOUT 26

WARM UP

PRE-FLEXIBILITY

MAIN WORKOUT

1. **Burpees** 2 sets of 15 reps
2. **Barbell squat with just the bar or light weight added**
   1 set of 15-20 reps.
3. **Barbell squat**
   4 sets of 8-10 reps
4. **Box jumps** 3 sets of 8-12 reps
5. **Superset – Kettlebell goblet box squat & one-legged box step ups/Box step-down**
   3 sets of supersets
   You will need a lower box for the goblet box squat and a taller box for the box step-ups and have them near enough together to do the exercise.
   As you squat down onto the box and squat back up, step onto the taller box with one leg, holding the kettlebell and squeeze your glutes when you are on the box, but avoid standing with the other leg. Then squat back down and then step up again with the opposite leg.

   Kettlebell goblet box squat & one-legged step-up combo
   10 reps
   Alternate each leg you step up with so you do 5 step-ups on each leg.
   Box step-downs 12 reps. 6 reps on each leg

COOLDOWN

POST-FLEXIBILITY

WORKOUT 27

WARM UP

PRE-FLEXIBILITY

MAIN WORKOUT

1. Superset – Lunge walk to one end of the room/ Side-walk back
   2 sets of supersets
2. Superset – Forward jump squats to one end of the room/ Forward high knees back
   2 sets of supersets
3. Sumo deadlift with just the bar or light weight added
   1 set of 15-20 reps
4. Superset – Sumo deadlift/Dumbbell glute bridge
   4 sets of supersets
   Sumo deadlift 8-12 reps
   Dumbbell glute bridge
   12 reps plus a 3-second hold after every rep
5. Superset – Barbell hip thrust/Bodyweight glute bridge hold
   4 sets of supersets
   Barbell hip thrust
   10-12 reps. 3-second hold between every rep
   Bodyweight glute bridge hold 15 seconds
6. Basic crunch
   4 sets of 45-second intervals
   30-second rest between sets

COOLDOWN

POST-FLEXIBILITY

WORKOUT 28

WARM UP

PRE-FLEXIBILITY

MAIN WORKOUT

1. Box step-ups
   1 set of 20 reps. Alternate each leg you step up with
2. Front squat with just the bar or light weight added
   1 set of 15 reps
3. Front squat 4 sets of 8-12 reps
4. Superset – Dumbbell squat/Mason twist
   4 sets of supersets
   Dumbbell squats 10 reps
   Mason twist 45 seconds
5. Dumbbell stationary lunge
   2 sets of 10-12 reps on each side/leg
6. Mountain climbers
   Intervals of 30 seconds on, 15 seconds off for 5 minutes

COOLDOWN

POST-FLEXIBILITY

WORKOUT 29

WARM UP

PRE-FLEXIBILITY

MAIN WORKOUT

1. **Burpees** 2 sets of 12 reps
2. **Romanian deadlift with just the bar or light weight added**
   1 set of 15 reps
3. **Superset – Romanian deadlift/Crab hip thrust**
   4 sets of supersets
   Romanian deadlifts 10-12 reps
   Crab hip thrust 12 reps
4. **Superset – Russian kettlebell swing/Mason twist**
   3 sets of supersets
   Russian kettlebell swing 15 reps
   Mason twist 45 seconds
5. **Double quadrupled hip abduction**
   2 sets of 12-15 reps on each side/leg
6. **Superset – Side-lying hip raise/Side plank**
   2 super sets on each side/leg
   Once you have done the side-lying hip raise, do the side plank on the same side/leg.
   Side-lying hip raise 12-15 reps
   Side plank 30-second hold

COOLDOWN

POST-FLEXIBILITY

WORKOUT 30

WARM UP

PRE-FLEXIBILITY

MAIN WORKOUT

1. **Bodyweight reverse lunge**
   2 sets of 12 reps on each side/leg. 4 sets in total
2. **Barbell squat with just the bar or light weight added**
   1 set of 20 reps
3. **Pyramids – Barbell squat**
   12 reps – 10 reps – 8 reps – 10 reps – 12 reps
4. **Stationary reverse lunge** 3 sets on each leg of 8-12 reps
5. **Hyperextensions** 3 sets of 8-12 reps
6. **Plank**
   4 sets of 45-second intervals
   30-second rest in between sets

COOLDOWN

POST-FLEXIBILITY

WORKOUT 31

WARM UP

PRE-FLEXIBILITY

MAIN WORKOUT

1. **Bodyweight lateral lunge**
   2 sets of 12-20 reps. Alternate each leg you lunge with
2. **Leg press with no weight or little weight added**
   1 set of 15-20 reps
3. **Pyramids – Leg press**
   15 reps – 12 reps – 9 reps – 6 reps – 9 reps – 12 reps – 15 reps
4. **Superset – Kettlebell Goblet box squat**
   & one-legged box step-ups/Box step-down
   You will need a smaller box for the goblet box squat and a taller box for the box step-ups and have them near enough together to do the exercise. As you squat down onto the box and squat back up, step onto the taller box with one leg, holding the kettlebell and squeeze your glutes when you are on the box but avoid standing with the other leg. Then squat back down and then step up again with the opposite leg.
   5 sets of supersets
   Kettlebell goblet box squat & one-legged step-up combo
   10 reps. Alternate each leg you step up with so you do
   5 step ups on each leg
   Box step-downs
   12 reps. 6 reps on each leg
5. **Mason twist** 3 sets of 45-second intervals
   15-second rest in between sets

COOLDOWN

POST-FLEXIBILITY

WORKOUT 32

WARM UP

PRE-FLEXIBILITY

MAIN WORKOUT

1. **Mountain climbers** 2 sets of 30-second intervals
2. **Barbell glute bridge** 4 sets of 8-12 reps
3. **Barbell hip thrust** 4 sets of 8-12 reps
4. **Hyperextensions** 3 sets of 8-12 reps
5. **Superset – Scorpion kick & Fire hydrant/ Scorpion kick pulse**
   2 supersets of 30-second intervals on both exercises on each side/leg. 30-second rest in between sets

   On the first exercise, do a Scorpion kick and then do a Fire hydrant. Remain doing the exercise on this leg/side for 30 seconds and then do the scorpion kick pulse on the same leg. Then do the same on the other leg.
6. **Superset – Side-lying leg raise/Side plank**
   3 supersets on each leg/side. After completing the side-lying leg raise, complete the side plank on the same side
   Side-lying leg raise 12-15 reps
   Side plank 30-second hold

COOLDOWN

POST-FLEXIBILITY

WORKOUT 33

WARM UP

PRE-FLEXIBILITY

MAIN WORKOUT

1. **Bodyweight glute bridge** 2 sets of 15 reps
2. **Stiff-legged deadlift with just the bar or light weight added**
   1 set of 15-20 reps
3. **Stiff-legged deadlift** 4 sets of 8-12 reps
4. **Superset – Dumbbell glute bridge/Goblet squat**
   4 sets of supersets
   Dumbbell glute bridge 10-12 reps
   Goblet squat 10-15 reps
5. **One-legged glute bridge**
   2 sets of 12 reps on each leg/side. 4 sets in total
6. **Superset – Calf-raised glute bridge/Reverse crunch**
   4 sets of supersets
   Calf-raised glute bridge 12 reps
   Reverse crunch 12-15 reps

COOLDOWN

POST-FLEXIBILITY

WORKOUT 34

WARM UP

PRE-FLEXIBILITY

MAIN WORKOUT

1. **Bodyweight stationary lunge**
   2 sets of 12 reps on each leg
2. **Superset – Jump squats/Wall squat with weight plate**
   4 sets of supersets
   Jump squat 12 reps
   Wall squat 45 seconds
3. **Barbell reverse lunge**
   5 sets of 12 reps. Alternate each leg you step back with so you are stepping back 6 times with each leg
4. **Box step-ups with dumbbells**
   3 sets of 12-20 reps. Alternate each leg you step up with
5. **Superset – Burpees/Plank**
   4 supersets of 30-second intervals on both exercises

COOLDOWN

POST-FLEXIBILITY

WORKOUT 35

WARM UP

PRE-FLEXIBILITY

MAIN WORKOUT

1. Bodyweight squat 1 set of 15 reps
2. Barbell hip thrust with just the barbell or light weight added 1 set of 15-20 reps
3. Barbell hip thrust 6 sets of 6-12 reps
4. Bodyweight Bulgarian split squat
   1 set of 12-15 reps on each side/leg. 2 sets in total
5. Dumbbell Bulgarian split squat
   2 sets of 8-12 reps on each side/leg. 4 sets in total
6. Bottoms up 3 sets of 45-second intervals

COOLDOWN

POST-FLEXIBILITY

WORKOUT 36

WARM UP

PRE-FLEXIBILITY

MAIN WORKOUT

1. **Mountain climbers** 2 sets of 30-second intervals
2. **Sumo deadlift with just the bar or light weight added**
   1 set of 15-20 reps
3. **Sumo deadlift** 6 sets of 6-10 reps
4. **Superset – Scorpion kick/Scorpion kick pulse**
   2 supersets on each side/leg. 4 supersets in total
   Scorpion kick 15 reps
   Scorpion kick pulse 15 pulses
5. **Fire hydrants**
   4 sets of 45-second intervals.
   Alternate each leg you raise on each set

COOLDOWN

POST-FLEXIBILITY

WORKOUT 37

WARM UP

PRE-FLEXIBILITY

MAIN WORKOUT

1. **Bodyweight reverse lunge**
   2 sets of 12 reps on each side/leg. 4 sets in total
2. **Barbell squat with just the bar or light weight added**
   1 set of 20 reps
3. **Pyramids – Barbell squat**
   12 reps – 10 reps – 8 reps – 10 reps – 12 reps
4. **Side-lying hip raise**
   3 sets of 12-15 reps on each side/leg. 4 sets in total
5. **Superset – side-lying leg raise/Side plank**
   3 supersets on each leg/side. After completing the side-lying leg raise, complete the side plank on the same side.
   Side-lying leg raise 12-15 reps
   Side plank 30-second hold

COOLDOWN

POST-FLEXIBILITY

WORKOUT 38

WARM UP

PRE-FLEXIBILITY

MAIN WORKOUT

1. **Bodyweight squat** 2 sets of 15 reps
2. **Barbell glute bridge with just the bar** 1 set of 15-20 reps
3. **Barbell glute bridge** 5 sets of 8-12 reps
4. **Superset – Kettlebell goblet box squat & one-legged box step-ups/ Box step-down**
   3 sets of supersets

   You will need a smaller box for the goblet box squat and a taller box for the box step-ups and have them near enough together to do the exercise. As you squat down onto the box and squat back up, step onto the taller box with one leg, holding the kettlebell and squeeze your glutes when you are on the box but avoid standing with the other leg. Then squat back down and then step up again with the opposite leg.

   Kettlebell goblet box squat & one-legged step up combo
   10 reps. Alternate each leg you step up with
   so you do 5 step-ups on each leg
   Box step-downs 12 reps. 6 reps on each leg
5. **Double quadrupled hip abduction**
   2 sets of 12-15 reps on each side/leg. 4 sets in total
6. **Bottoms up**
   2 sets of 45-second intervals. 20-second rest between sets

COOLDOWN

POST-FLEXIBILITY

EXERCISE INDEX

CABLE EXERCISES

PLYOMETRICS

RESISTANCE BANDS

ABDOMINAL/CORE EXERCISES

FLEXIBILITY/STRETCHING AND MOBILITY

POST-WORKOUT STRETCHES

SO THAT'S IT – THE COMPLETE BOOTYLICIOUS PROGRAMME!

HOW IS YOUR BOOTY LOOKING?

After your last workout, say out loud (or in your head if you're a little bit shy),

'I'M THE BOSS OF THIS PROGRAMME'

and give yourself a pat on the ASS! Take some pics and put them next to your before-programme pics. Have a look at how much you have changed with nothing but hard work and determination!

I am so proud of each one of you who has completed the whole programme. You should now have the confidence and determination to go at it alone and maybe even design your own workouts for yourself. Go on holiday, go for a night out and wear something to make your butt look booty-licous!

HAPPY BOOTY!

OTHER EXERCISES FOR YOUR GLUTES

Just because you are doing this training programme, it doesn't mean you can't do other sports and activities you enjoy! Try to fit the things you like doing in with the training programme.

Many sports make heavy use of the legs and buttocks, therefore helping to tone them, though they won't build as much muscle as squatting or deadlifting heavy. However, there is the added benefit that if you are working hard, you are burning fat.

CLIMBING/HIKING/SCRAMBLING

As you climb, you are heavily engaging your glutes as well as building endurance and strength. I always pick routes which are extra rocky and have large boulders as obstacles to climb over.

- Try to take BIG steps without putting yourself in danger.

If you don't live near any mountains, walking or jogging up steep hills will still engage your ass, hamstrings and calves. And for the extra work, squeeze that booty after every step!

CYCLING

Cycling, whether you are doing it indoors at a spin class or outside doing some recreational mountain biking, is an effective lower body and low impact workout. It strengthens and tones the glutes and legs and you do not realise how much you are using your ass until you feel it the next day! Opt for a class with heavy resistance or, if outdoors, a route which is very hilly. Your legs and bum will be working hard continuously.

SWIMMING

Swimming is an all-over body workout – and this includes working your butt! As you use your legs to move through the water, the water is acting as resistance which provides the legs with work and therefore helps strengthen them.

Kicking your legs whilst using a kick board and extending your arms in front of your body with one palm on top of the other will give your glutes a kick burn. Also, using the breaststroke kick and your legs wide heavily impacts your glutes due to the movement every time you bend, extend and bring your legs together. Your hip flexors are also greatly used. The freestyle kick is also an ideal method, whether you are in front-stroke or backstroke, for using your glute muscles as well as your hip flexors.

If you want to walk or jog through water, that's just as bootylicious for your booty. This is especially great if you are a weak swimmer or if you just want to keep your head above water. The water acts as added resistance to your legs and glutes as they execute the movement through the water. Running through water is far more challenging than you might think, though power walking through water would still be effective.

SKATING

Does this surprise you? Believe it or not, you actually work your glutes a lot more than you realise when skating. Think about it, you are using your legs and glutes to glide off from the start or when you put your foot down to add speed or to glide or move direction.

YOGA AND PILATES

If you regularly do yoga, then continue doing it. If you are keen to start, then start!

Yoga works the muscles in a different way, as it tones muscles all over the body. It relies on eccentric contraction, where muscles stretch as they contract. This increases flexibility in the muscles and joints. In general, yoga increases muscular endurance because you hold a pose for a certain length of time and repeat several times during a workout. Basically, yoga poses won't build the glutes like weightlifting will, but it will assist in giving a defined look. Yoga also strengthens and sculpts the core, which is always beneficial. There are many yoga poses that heavily target the glutes

Pilates also does a variety of good stuff to the body, such as building core strength, improving back health and improving daily posture. Like yoga, there are many ass-targeting poses from pilates.

I am not a yogi, but after researching, I have a list of some poses that will target your glutes. There will be more, but here's some to get you started.

Warrior I

Warrior II

Warrior III

Downward dog

Downward dog with leg extension

Chair pose

Locust pose

Yogic squat lifts

Pelvic tilt

Hamstring twist

Divers pose

Elevated wide squat

RUNNING

This can be running on a treadmill or outdoors, running in the woods. Some people say that cardio shrinks your butt. Many sports scientists advise that to build and maintain muscle growth whilst improving cardiovascular performance, opt for high-powered uphill running with shorter intervals and longer periods of rest/recovery.

Running can be included in other ways, such as during HIIT and outdoor boot camps. Remember, you are still putting pressure on the muscle, joints and anatomy of the hips and glutes. The glutes feel the burn when you run. They are the muscles that extend the hips, control rotation at the hip socket and stabilise you during running. If you love running, then carry on doing it, but incorporate it so it fits in with the shorter interval/longer recovery ratio.

ALTERNATIVE WAYS OF SAYING 'GLUTES'

To end this book, I've put together different things we call the buttocks. Some are more polite than others! Can you think of any others?

Ass ... Or AZZ
Arse ... UK version of Ass
Backpack
Backside
Badunkadonk ... A female with a small waist and high, round and juicy booty
Behind
Booty ... My favourite
Bubble Butt ... MMMMMMMM
Bum ... UK equivalent of butt
Buns ... As in a pair of buns (one butt cheek is one bun)
Butt ... US equivalent of bum
Butt Cheeks *(sometimes just called cheeks)*
Derriere ... Very polite way, used by the French
Donk
Fanny ... Used in the US (But beware – in the UK, fanny means vagina!)
Glutes ... Professional
Heinie
Jiggle-butt
Money-Maker
Pancake ... Insensitive way of describing someone's ass that is flat with no or next to no shape
Peach ... Normally a very positive way of describing a big, round and juicy ass
Posterior
Rear end
Shit bag ... I don't like this one!
Trunk ... Used in the popular Black Eyed Peas song, 'My Humps'
Tushy ... Probably the cutest way to describe an ass

BOOTY INSPIRATION

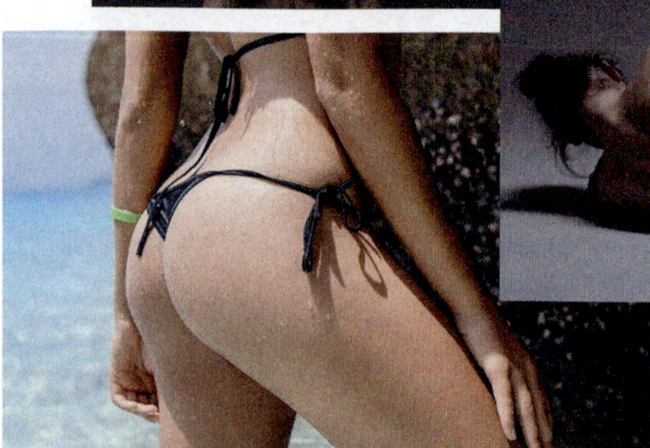

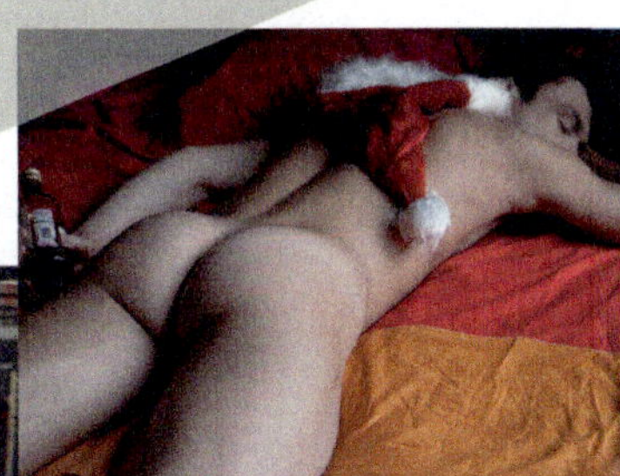

REFERENCES AND BACKGROUND INFORMATION

The author (that's me!) has made every effort to ensure the information provided in this book is as accurate and up to date as possible. The world in regard to fitness, medical and pharmaceuticals is constantly changing. I therefore cannot guarantee the information I have provided is 100% accurate. It is also recommended that readers consult a qualified medical specialist for their own individual medical advice. This book should not be used as an alternative to seeking specialist medical advice which should be sought prior to any action is taken.

The author and publisher cannot be held responsible for any errors and omissions found in the book, as well as any actions that may be taken by the reader as a result of any reliance on the information contained in the text which is taken entirely at the reader's risk.

Author: **Luke Boss**

Photography: **Jake Smith, Shutterstock**

Models: **Luke Boss, Jake Smith, Becky Rex**

Editor & proofreader: **Siân-Elin Flint-Freel**

REFERENCES

There's loads of information out there about exercise, diet and butts! Whilst writing this book, I found the following places to be really useful:

NHS website

Livestrong

AskMen

University of Buenos Aires

National library of medicine

www.bodybuilding.com

www.sci-mx.co.uk

Medicare

Lifetime Training – Where I achieved my qualifications. I learned in the classroom plus via the resources they provided me with. This is almost entirely where I learned about training and the components of it such as rep ranges and types of sets.

Printed in Great Britain
by Amazon

83728328R00147